Cross-Country Skiing

Cross-Country Skiing
Racing Techniques and Training Tips

By

SIGI MAIER
Instructor, Sports Center of the
Technical University of Munich

and

TONI REITER
Coach, German Ski Associaton

Translated by
Mark Goldman

Edited by
Don A. Metivier,
Executive Editor of *Ski Racing*

BARRON'S
Woodbury, N.Y.
London

Photograph facing title page:

A cross-country skier cutting through the woods.

All inquiries should be addressed to:
Barron's Educational Series, Inc.
113 Crossways Park Drive
Woodbury, New York 11797

Library of Congress Catalog Card No. 80-25026
International Standard Book No. 0-8120-2040-5

Library of Congress Cataloging in Publication Data

Maier, Sigi.
    Cross-country skiing.

    Translation of Skilanglauf heute.
    Includes index.
    1. Cross-country skiing. 2. Cross-country skiing—
Training. I. Reiter, Toni, joint author. II. Title.
GV855.3.M3413   796.93   80-25026
ISBN 0-8120-2040-5

PRINTED IN THE UNITED STATES OF AMERICA

Contents

Foreword by Don Metivier vii
Introduction viii
1. **Some Background Information** 1
   A Historical View 1
   Snow, Terrain, and Tracks 10
   Equipment and Clothing 14
   Roller Skiing 23

2. **The Health Benefits of Cross-Country Skiing** 25

3. **Waxing for Better Performance** 35
   General Importance of Waxing 35
   The Nature of Snow 36
   The Function of Wax 40
   Properties and Types of Waxes 43
   Waxing Accessories 49
   Preparation and Cleaning 49
   Waxing Your Skis 51
   Waxing for Races 56

4. **Cross-Country Ski Technique** 59
   Diagonal Striding 60
   The Fundamentals of Movement 68
   Pendulum Steps 89
   Double Poling 93
   Transitions 106
   Herringbone 110
   Skating Step 112
   Bow Step 115
   Bow Running 118
   Downhill Running 119
   Developing Technique and Style 128

5. **Training** 134
   Performance Factors—Conditioning 137
   Training Demands 140
   Cross-Country Training Methods 144
   Training Forms 149
   Tactics 160

Training Periods 161
Training Classes and Levels 165

6. The Thrill and Challenge of Competition 167

Racing Associations 167
Open Meets 169
Competition 177

7. Wilderness Skiing 189

References 193

Metric Conversion Table 193
The Olympic Record 193

Photographic Credits 196

Bibliography 197

Index 199

Foreword

by Don A. Metivier, executive editor of *Ski Racing,* the international journal of skiing, and past president of the U.S. Ski Writers Association

---

Cross-country skiing is a growth sport. Once the means of transportation for Scandinavians, it has developed throughout Europe and North America both as a popular form of exercise and as spirited competition.

Every skier taking part in competition, be it a Sunday-morning fun race with neighbors or a major international event, wants to do his or her best. New training methods have been developed over the past few years that permit these weekend skiers to improve times while also allowing national team skiers to become more competitive.

The best of these training methods have come from Germany. These new training procedures are presented here in *Cross-Country Skiing,* making these highly respected and sophisticated German training programs available to American skiers for the first time. Sigi Maier and Toni Reiter explain how the length of training runs, the build-up of lactic acid in the body, the change of intensity in workouts, and the importance of pulse rate are all vital parts of the overall training process. They show how to increase the effectiveness of every cross-country movement, and discuss how important appropriate waxing is for smoother, faster skiing.

Cross-Country Skiing provides important information for any skier wanting to improve performance, whether it be in a local ski club program, school course, or organized race, at any of the many levels of competition available in the United States and Canada.

Introduction

"Länglaufer leben langer" is a popular German slogan that can be seen on ski caps, on bumper stickers, and on tee-shirts throughout Europe. It translates to "Cross-country skiers live longer," and it points to one of the main reasons for the tremendous recent growth in cross-country skiing, in both Europe and North America. The sport has blossomed because it offers basic good exercise, easy mastery of skills, and a lower cost than the ever-more-expensive Alpine form of skiing.

And as the sport has increased in popularity, so has the number of skiers interested in competition. The long-neglected Nordic ski teams of Europe and North America have begun to get more attention. In recent years many formerly Alpine-oriented nations have begun funding and training cross-country ski teams as well. The future holds only promise of even greater attention to this sport.

For years, success in Nordic ski competition had been monopolized by the Scandinavians. Their prominence in the area dates back to the very origins of the sport. Until 1956, when a Russian won a bronze medal in the popular men's 15-kilometer Olympic race, only skiers from Norway, Finland, or Sweden had ever finished in the top three places. The Soviets made great gains in Nordic strength, and then the Germans began developing new training techniques for cross-country competition. The East Germans led the way, trying out training programs that had their skiers successfully challenging the long-standing Scandinavians. These training techniques were honed, improved, and adopted by other European countries, and soon the new methods were recognized as the key to cross-country racing success. Many of these training methods have now been adopted by Western coaches. They have been used by North American teams as well, with success.

Cross-Country Skiing provides a European training program for individual skiers in this country. Not readily available before, this training program applies the winning principles developed by those European countries that have been successful getting the edge on the Scandinavians. It is hoped that this book will help dedicated skiers to reach the level of excellence they seek. For those becoming interested in the growing numbers of competitions, the techniques and principles propounded here will show the way toward achieving those medals. It must be noted, however, that no training program will succeed without the hard work and dedication of talented athletes. Should you have this talent and dedication, the challenge and excitement of cross-country racing await you.

Some Background Information

A Historical View

To those in countries where Alpine, or downhill, skiing has been the most popular snow sport, cross-country skiing is a relatively new phenomenon. As late as the middle '60s it was basically unknown, seen at best as a difficult sport for panting, sweat-bathed Nordic types possessed by some unfathomable drive. During the '70s, however, cross-country skiing became increasingly popular. As lift lines became longer, ticket prices higher, and equipment more sophisticated and expensive, many people turned to the simpler way of skiing. There was a rediscovery of a centuries-old method of transportation, which is also one of the oldest and most natural forms of sport.

The problem of traveling over snow was first encountered by peoples living in the northern latitudes, who were forced to hunt in the winter for their survival. The problem was first resolved by the invention of snowshoes, which enlarged the surface area of the foot, thereby preventing a person from sinking into the snow. Gliding, a faster means of travel, was made possible by the further refinement of the snowshoe to produce the ski—presumably some 5,000 years ago.

Skis, as well as snowshoes, were probably first developed in central Asia and introduced, via Russia, to Scandinavia. It is there that one finds the most significant indications of age, technical development, and use of skis. Surprisingly enough, skis were improved there to a degree of sophistication that rivals our present-day standards.

Substantive proof for the use of skis by Stone Age hunters is found in cave drawings. The oldest of these, believed to be approximately 5,000 years old, was discovered in 1927 on the Norwegian island of Rodoy. It shows a hunter in a rabbit mask on a pair of very long skis with bowed, elongated tips. In the bogs of Scandinavia, peat cutters have found over a hundred skis in good condition, the oldest of which has been estimated to be approximately 4,500 years old. In similar finds dating from the Bronze and Iron ages, skis with such modern features as running grooves, raised tips, and toe-clamp straps made of animal tendons have been uncovered. After the transition from a hunting to a farming society, the Scandinavians retained the ski as an important tool for their existence during the long snowy winters; in fact, it was a necessary part of their livelihood.

In Greek and Roman histories one finds reports of snowshoes or skis (for example, Xenophon, 400 B.C.). Written histories first appeared in Scandinavia in the twelfth and thirteenth centuries (Heimskringla, Edda). From histories and myths (and from the border area between the two) we hear of heroes, kings, even gods who wore skis. For example, the Norwegian King Harald I is reputed to have executed one of his subjects for being a more accomplished skier. Whereas in warmer lands a sun god was honored, the northerners honored a ski god and goddess: Ull and Skade, respectively. Many place names are derived from these two deities, even the inclusive name *Scandinavia,* which is a reference to the goddess of skiers, illustrating the importance of skiing.

Historical events lend an almost political significance to the ski. One of the most famous ski stories of all time dates back to a civil war underway in Norway in the early part of the thirteenth century. King Sverrir sent two of his most trusted scouts, called "birchlegs," to carry his infant son to safety. They traveled about thirty-five miles in the midst of a heavy storm with the baby, who later became the great King Haakon IV. The annual Birkebeiner race is still held in Norway to commemorate this dash to safety of skis. There is also an annual Birkebeiner race in the United States in Wisconsin. The winner qualifies to ski in the Norwegian race.

Another event that has remained a part of modern ski lore took place in 1522. The young Swedish revolutionary and noble, Gustav Eriksson, was fleeing his country when he was stopped by his followers at Sälen, only fifteen miles from the Norwegian border. They convinced him to return, raised an army, and later elected him King Gustav I. Vasa. The 85-kilometer Vasaloppet Cross-Country race marks this bit of skiing history; it is an annual race from Sälen to Mora in northern Sweden. Recently an international Loppet League was formed to coordinate long-range cross-country races all over the world.

In 1555 Olaus Magnus, bishop of Uppsala in central Sweden, wrote a significant work on the culture and history of the peoples of the North, which contained many references to skis in history. He reported, for example, that the Laplanders used skis not only for hunting, but also for competitions and downhill skiing. He also mentioned the one-pole method. Although the book reached the continent and is credited with introducing the news of skiing there, it made no lasting impression. This was to happen later, as a result of another book.

The Development of Sport

The next major development in Scandinavia came during the nineteenth century, when skiing developed much more into a sport. At that time, in Telemark, a mountainous region of south-central Norway, skiing experienced a resurgence that led to the modern-day sport. Developing a technique that bore the region's name, Norwegians improved the ski by shaping, tapering, and refining it and by developing heel and toe straps. Telemarkers considered skiing their favorite pastime, and they soon developed a series of competitions. The first timed cross-country ski race is believed to have been run in Telemark in 1848, with the winner covering the 5-kilometer distance in just under thirty minutes.

The first cross-country ski race in Oslo, at Iverslokken, was held in 1866. Sondre Norheim, a ski pioneer from Telemark, went to Christiania—present-day Oslo—in 1868 to ski in that race. He used his excellent technical skills to develop another ski technique, the Christiania turn, and in Oslo he was looked on as a wizard. Thus Christiania and Telemark became the techniques of the day, and skiing as sport boomed.

In 1887, using two poles—rather than one, as in the early Telemark method—became popular. By 1890 skis especially designed for racing were introduced. A new "mousetrap" binding was used in 1892—the beginnings of the bindings in use today. And the first ski waxes were introduced during the winter of 1903. By this time skiing had made such headway as a sport that in 1910 a cross-country race was held in Finland that was just for women.

Meanwhile, the race at Iverslokken continued, and on Wednesday February 12, 1879, about 10,000 spectators watched as jumping was added. The cross-country and jumping events were the direct forerunners of the Holmenkollen. In 1892, the new jumping site at Holmenkollen was first put into use, and in 1979, the 100th anniversary of this Holmenkollen race was celebrated.

Although Bishop Magnus' book introduced skiing to the rest of Europe, it was another book, published more than 300 years later, that actually popularized the sport. In 1888, the Norwegian

Fridtjof Nansen crossed Greenland on skis. He wrote an account of this feat, and in 1891 it was translated into English, French, and German. That same year the first German ski club, Todtnau, was organized.

Early German ski championships were held in Feldberg in 1900, but because of the region's mountainous nature, Alpine skiing gained tremendous popularity and there were relatively few cross-country skiers; their meager competitions were virtually ignored.

Just the opposite was true in Scandinavia, however. There, three-quarters of the population regularly used cross-country skis, and thousands of people attended the competitions that featured Nordic events. Scandinavians—first the Norwegians, then the Swedes, and later the Finns—dominated international cross-country ski competition.

Skiing was introduced to the United States by Norwegians who were brought to the country to work the mines. Many of them wound up in California during the gold rush years, and they spent much of their time ski racing for buckets of beer, using skis that were as much as twelve feet long and weighing about twenty-five pounds.

A lad who was born in the birthplace of skiing, Jon Thoresen Rue, was brought by his parents from Telemark to California in 1837. He grew up as John A. "Snowshoe" Thomson, and he gained lasting fame for carrying mail, at $2 a letter, from Placerville, California, on the western side of the Sierra Nevadas to Genoa, Nevada. He worked for thirteen winters, quitting in 1869 when the Union Pacific completed a railroad that would replace him.

Skiing grew in the middle west of the United States through the efforts of other Scandinavians who settled there. Most of these people thought real skiers were ski jumpers, and so that part of the sport really grew during the early years of the twentieth century.

Eastern colleges stepped in and began forming outing clubs that sponsored cross-country skiing. The first of these, the famed Dartmouth Outing Club, was formed on December 7, 1909, at Hanover, New Hampshire. Other colleges followed suit and soon ski competition began.

Skiing even moved indoors. In the 1930s, major ski exhibitions were held in arenas, attracting huge crowds, the largest of which was at New York City's old Madison Square Garden. The staging of the 1932 Winter Olympic Games at Lake Placid, New York, also helped increase the popularity of cross-country skiing in the United States.

While World War II put skiing on a back burner for several years, it also provided the personnel for most of the development that has brought cross-country to its popular level today. Recognizing the need for ski troops, the military formed the Tenth Mountain Division, which was trained at Camp Hale in Colorado. The ski troopers gained fame for opening the main route to Rome when they invaded the Po Valley and captured Riva Ridge. One of the officers, Pete Siebert, later named a ski run at the resort he founded after the war (Vail, Colorado) after that famous battle. One of his skiers, Penny Tweedy, named a race horse after the ski run; Riva Ridge went on to be a winner of the Kentucky Derby.

The veterans of the Tenth Mountain Division were everywhere in the ski business after the war, and they started most of the major ski resorts. They developed the big hotels, taught and refined the sport, and wrote about skiing or made films of it. It was largely their efforts that helped make skiing one of the growth sports of the second half of the twentieth century in this country.

Cross-country skiing is an ideal sport for women.

Cross-country skiing can be practiced with surprising success by the physically handicapped as well. This one-armed skier, winner of several world championships for the handicapped, is also competitive in the large international open meets. He was, for example, in the top 100 out of 2,000 participants in a 60-kilometer race.

Cross-country skiers stay young longer. An excellent example of this is Walter Demel, shown here winning his fortieth German championship at forty years of age. ▽

Cross-country skiing is aesthetically pleasing.

Growing Competition

In the beginning all the winners were Scandinavians, but when cross-country skiing really started to catch on, other nations found they had winners in their ranks. The first cross-country champion from Central Europe was Hans Beraur of Czechoslovakia who, in 1939, won the combined world championship—a pairing of jumping and cross-country events. And by the middle of the twentieth century, the Soviets began to really pull the medals away from the Scandinavians.

The Soviet men did well, especially in the relays and in longer distances when Viatches Vedenin and Pavel Kolchin burst on the international scene. However it was the Soviet women who really dominated cross-country competition at this time. In the

Competition for the elite: the 1976 Olympia.

Some 10,000 skiers competed in the Engadiner Skimarathon.

women's 10-kilometer Olympic event, Soviet women won a gold and a bronze medal in 1956, then swept all medals in 1960 and 1964. They were almost as victorious in the 5-kilometer events.

Galina Koulakova was the best of the Soviet women, earning a total of eight world titles, then coming back in 1979 at age thirty-six to win the World Cup. She is called the "Champion of Champions" among women Nordic skiers.

Shortly after the Soviets began their sweeping victory, other nations started to develop winners. The first German cross-country combined champion in international competition soon came along. He was Georg Thoma, and he won the 1960 Olympic gold medal in games held at Squaw Valley, California.

That breakthrough helped cross-country skiing gain even more in popularity worldwide and attract increasing numbers of athletes from the continent. These athletes began to narrow the differences in times between themselves and the Scandinavians. At the same time there was a parallel growth in general enthusiasm for cross-country skiing, and the development of new training programs that were to bring even more success to European cross-country competitors in world class events.

While major competition was increasing in Europe, another important development—the introduction of ski touring for recreational skiers—brought many more people into the sport. On January 31, 1965, the Munich Invitational Ski Meet, the first of its type in the Alpine regions, launched touring on a major scale. The meet was a huge success even though, or perhaps because, it coincided with a wave of enthusiasm for Alpine skiing that swept Europe and the United States.

Cross-country skiing had a few years of mild success, then in the 1970s it experienced a breathtaking increase in popularity,

In high elevations there is never a problem with snow.

the end of which is still not in sight. The number of tourers, light tourers, and racers all increased. Many more events were organized; training programs were developed at the sports academies. And then manufacturers took notice. Soon new, sophisticated equipment reached the marketplace and a fashionable sport was molded.

Why Cross-Country?

For many, cross-country skiing was less expensive than Alpine skiing, it was a sport easily and quickly learned, it offered a life-long interest, it was comparatively safe, and it certainly was healthy and good for the body. These were reasons enough to spend time cross-country skiing.

Others, however, saw cross-country skiing as an exciting and demanding new sport. They wanted to strain their bodies, wipe stinging sweat from their eyes, feel their hearts pounding in their chests, sense blood pumping furiously through their veins, and extend themselves in a challenge to others. It created a constant desire to race, to excel, and this led to the establishment of entirely new conditioning and training schedules. Skiers found they had to learn more about their sport. Knowledge of terrain, snow, waxes, equipment, conditioning, and training were now necessary parts of the sport for serious skiers who wanted to compete.

Snow, Terrain, and Tracks

Snow, terrain, and tracks are indispensable factors for cross-country skiing. They are necessary parts of the training and skiing experience, and an understanding of the role of each is necessary for the serious skier.

Snow

Snow is to the cross-country skier what water is to a fish or music to a musician—absolutely necessary! While the Alpine skier must worry about the quantity of snow, the quality of snow is what is crucial to the cross-country skier. Most important is the type of surface.

Although recent breakthroughs in wax technology and even the development of waxless skis have enabled skiers to use all types of snow, there are different surface conditions with which skiers should become familiar. Quick gliding motions are possible when the snow surfaces consist of cold powder, cold granular or frozen snow, or moist granular snow. On the other hand, there may be more problems in waxing if you are dealing with any rapidly changing snow surface; fresh snow with above-freezing temperatures; wet snow; or the melting, soft "mashed-potato" snow of spring.

In the Northeast, snow can become very hard. Frozen granular snow to an eastern skier is ice to a westerner used to

The dream of every cross-country skier: every winter should be like this.

A properly cut trail: hip-wide and consistently parallel.

plenty of fresh powder. Eastern skiers will get some powder from time to time, but the East is known for its hard-packed, well-used surfaces, while the West is attractive for its seemingly endless supply of fresh powder. In the Midwest, skiers take what they can get or what they make.

Terrain

Cross-country skiers can use nearly any snow-covered area for a track. The ideal terrain is rolling, open meadows; forest paths; or any combination of these two. The mixed terrain provides interesting, changing surfaces that enable skiers to use all their techniques.

Most skiers have to make do with the terrain that exists where they are. Only the well-financed national teams can chase the snow or select the choice terrain, and they find that difficult at best. Whereas Alpine skiers might train in South America or Australia off-season, Nordic skiers use roller skis wherever they might be. They hope for a national camp in Durango or Telemark, where they make snow for cross-country skiing.

Make use of the best terrain available to you, whether you be training on snow or on roller skis. In winter, high school teams use golf courses, and college teams set tracks around their campus. Dartmouth, for example, skis around Hanover and back across the quad. Since there is no commercial attraction in cross-country skiing, no enterprising souls are making snow for this sport.

Tracks

While skiing through fresh-fallen snow can be enjoyable and making your own tracks in new snow a challenge, the best training can be done on a prepared track. Fresh, untracked snow sometimes allows the ski to sink too deeply for gliding and makes constant lifting and walking necessary. In contrast, skiing on a completely frozen surface permits no penetration of the ski edges, and skiing in a wet track can result in damage to skis and boots, not to mention wet feet for the skier.

Whenever possible, your training routines should be done on surfaces that would normally be found on race courses. The ideal condition is loose, dry, light snow or a firm surface that allows the ski to grab while striding. Or find the very best of tracks—a base of granular snow with a thin covering of fresh powder.

Nearly all tracks are now made by track-setting equipment, and skiers will find most courses uniform. The tracks provide an individual groove of the proper depth for each ski. There are also a firm bottom to the tracks and firm sides of each groove, set about hip-width, with a steady division of snow between the

Without a track, deep snow can be too much of a good thing.

In this case, cutting your own track is truly enjoyable.

grooves and a firm track on both sides for the poles.

Skiers wanting to set their own tracks should remember these helpful tips:

- Always cut the tracks hip-width because too narrow or too wide a track results in unnatural posture and poor balance.

- Always keep skis parallel.

- On compact snow, set the track with slow, careful, short, and firm steps. Go over the course a few times.

- If the snow is loose and deep, cut a track and then pack it by side-stepping the course, using two skiers facing in opposite directions. This method is doubly efficient since it also prepares a firm bed for the poles. Once the track has been packed by side-stepping, cut the final track carefully and glide into it.

A special tractor cuts tracks for skiing.

Equipment and Clothing

The innovations in cross-country ski equipment developed over the past few years are amazing. As more people took up the sport, more ski manufacturers started looking seriously at this market. Firms that had never manufactured cross-country skis but had been giants in the downhill industry now recognized the opportunity in the cross-country market and began making some excellent products.

This boom made the manufacture of cross-country skis, and other ski equipment as well, much more competitive. It resulted in a great deal more research and development in the field. Waxless skis, looked at with scorn by purists, suddenly took on new importance when an American—Billy Koch—skied with them to his nation's first Nordic Olympic medal. Koch took second place in the men's highly competitive 30-kilometer event in the 1976 Olympic Games at Seefeld, Austria. (The games were officially held in Innsbruck, but the Nordic events were contested at Seefeld, a few miles away.)

Another major breakthrough came at Lake Placid in the 1980 Winter Games, as new waxes were used for the first time and the first Olympic cross-country competition was held on man-made snow. The continuing expansion of the cross-country market assures skiers a wide range of new skis, boots, and wax products from manufacturers eager to gain or hold a portion of the suddenly lucrative Nordic business.

The selection of equipment is a very personal thing, especially for the experienced skier and racer. Skiers are bombarded with information on all types of skis, boots, poles, and bindings. Every company of any size publishes catalogs. Consumer ski magazines conduct annual tests on new equipment and publish their results. Skiers do not lack information on what new equipment is available. However, the best information skiers can have is that of how the equipment performs for them: how the skis respond, how waxes hold up in changing snow conditions, which boots are comfortable on their feet.

Manufacturers realize that such elements are important. Most of them make demonstrator models available to dealers or company reps, who travel the race circuit and visit the major touring centers. You should try as much new equipment as possible to determine which ones are best for your personal skiing style.

Some of the following information on equipment will help you make the important decisions.

Ski types: *top:* special (racing) ski; *middle:* special (training) ski; *bottom:* light touring ski.

Skis

While learning the sport, most beginners choose a *touring* ski. It performs best on a prepared track, is wider and heavier than a racing ski, tapers from front to back, is flexible, and has a well-defined groove that holds the snow. *Racing* skis are very light, have little taper, are lively with tension in the middle (cambered), and are very responsive.

There are also many types of skis. *Waxless* skis, such as those with fishscale, mohair, and concave-negative bottoms, have become increasingly popular. New developments in skis are reaching the marketplace each season. *Wax* skis are also changing. The amount of area to be waxed, fiberglass and wood bottoms, and wet- or powder-snow camber are but a few of the many options available.

Racers who had paid little or no attention to waxless skis soon discovered that they were acceptable for conditions that otherwise presented severe waxing problems; in some cases, they were the only sure way to avoid missing the wax of the day.

It is difficult to get a strong kick from waxless skis on a frozen granular or icy track, and the glide from a correctly waxed ski on hard, cold powder snow is normally much better than from a waxless model. However, the waxless ski is now very much a part of the ski-racing scene.

When purchasing skis, don't overlook one of the most important criteria. Be sure the skis have the correct tension or camber for your particular needs. A ski that is not properly matched to your weight will not perform correctly. If the ski is too soft, or the body weight too great for the camber, the center section will be pushed down on the snow, creating a drag. The wax layer will wear away faster, quickly lowering the climbing and kicking potential of the ski. If, however, a ski is too hard or the body weight too little for the camber, then not even a hard kick will cause the surface under the foot to make firm contact with the snow surface, again diminishing the kicking and climbing power.

The difficulty in matching skis to individual skiers has increased because of the development of synthetic skis, which have ranging tension zones. The center of the ski—the climbing zone—is more flexible and is waxed with climbing wax. The front and rear sections of the ski—the glide zones—are waxed with glide wax. Ideally the climbing zone should come in contact with the snow only during the kick. In the glide, the ski must support the skier's weight, allowing only the glide zones to contact the snow. Therefore it is more important than ever that skiers find skis that provide the proper balance between body weight and ski tension to insure that the ski will function properly.

You should test every pair of skis you use to be sure the correct tension for your body weight is present. When purchasing skis, be sure there are no defects and that the skis are a perfectly matched pair. Check the skis carefully for warping and irregularities in the grooves and width. Place the skis bottom-to-bottom and push them together in the center. The glide zones should be tightly pressed to one another. Bowing the shovel—the front of the ski—should create a long, even curve.

Bindings

For years the "mousetrap" binding, which fastened the boots to the skis at the toes, allowed the heel vertical freedom while preventing lateral movement. This was all that was needed for cross-country skiing. In recent years, however, manufacturers

Above left: light touring ski with a large area on bottom surface covered with fish scales; *right:* racing ski with smaller area covered with fish scales and without center groove.
Below: detail of the bottom of a fish-scale ski.

Mohair skis.

have made changes in Nordic bindings, just as they have in the very sophisticated Alpine bindings. Still, the purpose of the bindings remains the same: keep the boot attached to the ski and allow vertical freedom for the kick and the climb.

Decide on a binding only after you have chosen your boots, since the holding mechanism must be compatible with the boot design. Heel plates have become popular, insuring that the boot will be held firmly in place and free of lateral movement when the snow is flat on the ski.

Binding assemblies vary from type to type and whoever installs them must closely follow the mounting instructions. Generally the center of the binding should be attached to the gravitational center of the ski. Care must be taken to find both centers so as to distribute equally the weight of the ski. Use only the drill size specified, since too large a drill will make the holes

An instrument for measuring the tension of skis.

One-piece bindings: *left:* (old) Nordic Norm;
right: symmetrical plastic side supports.

too big for the screws to grip. If the drill is too small, the screws will be too tight, causing the surface lamination of the ski to crack. And, be careful not to drill too deeply.

Boots

Boot manufacturers have also made technological advances in the past few seasons, and cross-country skiers have a great variety of footgear from which to choose. Good boots must be lightweight, have flexible soles that do not allow the heel to bend out, and have some soft material over the toes to help avoid blisters. They should fit well, with room in the tip so your toes don't get cold, and also have a firm fit in the heel.

Despite the development of many synthetic materials, the best boots still have uppers made of leather and a sole of a strong man-made material. This allows the skier the excellent qualities of a fine leather boot, with the further advantage of a strong sole that transfers the kick from the boot to the ski more efficiently.

Racing boots are cut low and are very light. Cross-country

Note size comparison between old and new Nordic Norm.

Modern "beak" bindings, fastened with a pin.

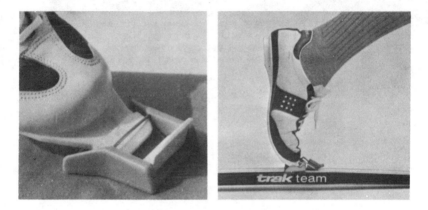

Binding fastened with a metal bar.

Binding offers maximum mobility for the kick phase.

touring boots are available in low or high cuts, with the higher models providing more ankle support and also being warmer.

Take care of all your equipment, including protecting leather boots from moisture. There are a great variety of excellent leather-care products on the market, and cross-country boots should be treated both before use and during the season.

Poles

Poles are a very important part of the cross-country skier's equipment. They are used on every kick of the ski, and, in racing, they must be strong enough to sustain double-poling techniques from skiers who ask a lot of their equipment.

The most recent development in poles has been the carbon-fiber shaft, which is very lightweight, strong, and

Modern racing boots with "beak" for bindings with three studs.

For bindings with metal bar fastening, new Nordic Norm.

long-lasting but very expensive. Work on pole development continues, and annual consumer guides point out new shaft materials as they become available.

Handgrips for cross-country are also changing, as they have for Alpine poles. Most skiers still like a strap on the grip, and the development of the wider outside strap has been an improvement. The wider strap helps skiers avoid painful blisters, and it transfers arm movement to the poles from the grip.

Tips of the poles must grip in even the hardest snow, yet still be easy to retrieve. Many fine-quality poles have the bottom section angled forward to aid in planting on an icy trail.

The traditional round basket on the poles has given way to many new versions, all with the same purpose: to keep the pole from sinking too deeply into snow alongside the tracks.

You should try all types of poles, tips, and baskets, then select the combination best suited for your style of skiing. Poles should reach to the armpit, with the tips on solid ground.

Earlier racing boot—today suitable only for training.

Ankle-high touring boots.

Clothing

Cross-country clothing must be lightweight, fit well, and protect you from wind and cold, yet also allow the body heat created by physical exertion to be released. Most coaches and trainers recommend thin layers of clothing. They urge skiers not to overdress with warm parkas that are fine for riding lifts but not for the heavy exercise of skiing.

For many years cross-country skiers would only be seen in knickers, high socks, and a lightweight cotton jacket with tight-fitting cuffs and a high collar. Then manufacturers introduced jumpsuits and these became very popular. Knee-length versions of jumpsuits were joined by ankle-length suits, and it wasn't long before fashion designers began developing designs for cross-country skiers. National racing teams were now provided with colorful and practical uniforms and training clothing. The trend to more fashionable cross-country clothing will continue, now that there is such a good market for it.

Underwear is also very important. It must be light, warm, nonirritating, and absorbent. Underwear should allow air out while absorbing sweat from the body, as should socks.

Because you have to grip the poles, you'll find gloves more practical than mittens. Here again new designs have developed. Leather gloves have given way to synthetic materials, and

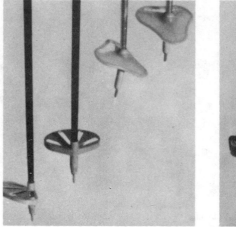

Modern pole tips:
slightly angled
Widia tips, full and
half baskets.

Pole grip with a
wide, adjustable
strap.

super-warm gloves of very thin material now provide warmth for the coldest of ski days, as well as offering a good feel for the grip on the poles.

Skiers who spend long periods of time in very cold temperatures or in heavy snow will find the once-popular gaiters are still good protection against wet, cold feet. These extra covers do not fit all types of boots, however.

Synthetic boot covering to protect against moisture.

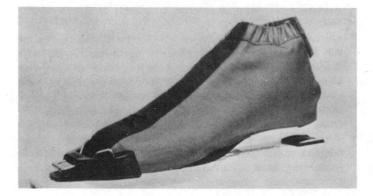

Roller Skiing

For many years cross-country skiers had to give up their sport in the snowless summer and fall. Many rode bikes, played soccer, and ran to keep their legs in shape, all of which provided excellent exercise. Recently, however, the development of roller skis has allowed skiers to use the techniques of their sport throughout the year.

Roller skis have hard rubber wheels attached to a wooden shaft. They hold a cross-country boot in place with a binding. When used with poles, the roller skis provide a very similar experience to snow skiing. They are usually used on roads and other paved surfaces.

In order to grip blacktop and other hard surfaces, a Widia tip should be used on the poles. And skiers found that they got sore arms and shoulders from long periods of planting the poles on hard surfaces, so a shock-absorber pole was developed. If you plan to roller ski on a regular basis as part of an off-season training program, use this new equipment to ease the strain.

Roller-ski training sessions are held on a regular basis by most national ski teams and by many college squads. There are also summer races to provide competition. The sport is growing each year.

Roller skis: *top:* aluminum ski with antislip device on the front; *bottom:* wooden skis with antislip device at the back and brakes.

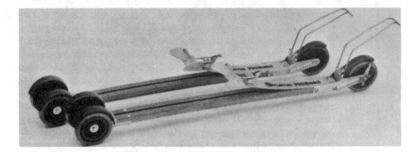

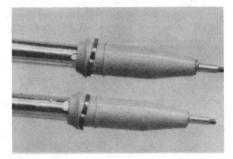

Roller ski poles with telescopic suspension and Widia tips.

The Health Benefits
of Cross-Country Skiing

As was mentioned earlier in this book, the latest, and some of the most successful, cross-country training methods have been developed in Germany. Part of the reason for this has been the tremendous interest in exercise and its health benefits, particularly as they relate to competition. Much medical research has been done on exercise and its relation to health by such outstanding facilities as the Research Center of the German Sport Federation.

The following is one of the best compilations of this data now available, a paper written by Dr. H.P. Heynen, team doctor for the German Ski Association. Dr. Heynen did most of his work at the Federation's Research Center, and his information is very detailed. It should be of great benefit to the skier seeking the reasons for and the results of heavy training and exercise.

Cross-country skiing is a pure endurance sport. According to present-day standards, sports such as cross-country ski racing over distances ranging from 5 kilometers for women (time: approximately 15 minutes) to the men's 50-kilometer marathon (time: 2 to 3 hours) to the open competitions of more than 90 kilometers (time: 5 to 10 hours) are classified as long-endurance sports. Even noncompetitive light tourers often ski for at least an hour on a simple outing.

Whenever one sees a skier gliding effortlessly along on a pair of well-waxed skis on a good track, the fluid motions of his or her diagonal technique illustrate clearly that cross-country skiing is a classic example of a dynamic, rhythmic sport. It also becomes clear that, in addition to the demands placed on the inner organs, the entire body is in constant motion. Because of the glide phase, no one part of the body is overexerted. There are only a few other sports that possess this positive characteristic.

The demands placed on the entire body are especially noticeable in the limbs. The demands on the legs, hips, and other parts of the lower torso owing to the striding motion are obvious. Because of the simultaneous use of poles, the arms and upper torso are also working, so that the entire body from the fingertips to the toes is exercised. That the toes and fingertips are used is clearly seen in the final motions preceding the change from the glide phase to the kick phase. The outstretched fingertips maintain contact with the pole. In the kick, the foot rolls all the way up onto the ball of the foot before the leg shoots back.

Because the demands on the body's musculature are primarily endurance oriented, although there are clearly elements of strength and speed required, the body does not become overly developed. This is not to say that the body's muscles do not increase in size. The shoulders, hips, thighs, and calves will become visibly larger. Cross-country skiers tend to be athletically built: thin but well developed.

Since the developing muscles are used to propel the body forward with little need for braking movements, the less flexible parts of the body—the ligaments, tendons, cartilage, and bones—are not subjected to excessive wear and tear. This is, however, not the case with summer training.

Depending upon the lay and length of the course, the constant demand on the body's musculature in general and on those muscle groups used for climbing or downhill runs is at a relatively high level. And the organs that supply the body's energy—the heart, the circulatory system, and the lungs—are under constant pressure. This results in measurable improvements in the body's general condition. Of these improvements, the most well known and well documented in endurance sports are those found in the heart and circulatory system.

An enlargement of the heart—the so-called athlete's heart, with its low heartbeat, pulse rate, and blood pressure at rest, as well as an increase of maximum rates—is characteristic of the increase in overall capacity. The volume of the heart of a normal individual who is not active in sports is approximately 10 cubic centimeters per kilo of body weight. This ratio increases to 14 to 16 (sometimes even 18) cubic centimeters per kilo for top racers. A low pulse rate, generally around 40 per minute, as well as lowered blood pressure (110/90), is common among skiers. These are not, however, solely owing to training at an intensive level. The central nervous system may also influence these organs. A better indicator of improved body condition is a comparison of the pulse rate and blood pressure after strenuous activity. These should return to normal one to two minutes after the activity is completed.

The pulse rate and blood pressure of a cross-country skier should be lower than those of an inactive person of the same age under equal stress. Younger skiers, depending upon the intensity and level of their training, have expanded their heart volume to over 200 cubic centimeters. "Older" skiers who have skied for years do not, however, show this increase in heart volume.

The lungs supply the body with oxygen, which is very important in the production of energy. Together with the heart and circulatory systems, the lungs are important organs for endurance sports. The lung capacity of a well-conditioned skier is far superior to that of an inactive person. The capacity can be increased to 7 liters, which equals 100 cubic centimeters per kilo of body weight. The maximum intake possible is clearly greater than a normal person's: between 150 and 200 liters per minute. Once again, if compared to a normal person under normal stress, the skier should need less air as a result of his conditioning.

The oxygen consumption of the musculature during skiing is more important than the metabolic rate. The achievements of an athlete are measured by the amount of work he gets from his

Open meets for children are not uncommon in Scandinavian countries.

This man, over sixty years old, has just completed a 60-kilometer course.

muscles. The heart, circulatory system, and lungs are important but cannot produce results without the attached musculature. A distinctive characteristic of the well-conditioned athlete is a decreased oxygen consumption in comparison to that of an inactive individual. It is important to understand in connection with this that it is not the method but rather the intensity of training that causes increased oxygen consumption in the musculature. This can be achieved only by exceeding the normal rate in training as often as possible. This causes an increase in the production of enzymes, oxygen converters, energy-rich phosphates, and cells, which in turn increase the oxygen consumption rate. Endurance training at a less intensive level does not have this effect.

Just as the supply and consumption of oxygen must be increased, so must the concentration of energy sources in the muscles. These are basically fats and carbohydrates and their by-products—fatty acids and glucose. One of the characteristics of muscles that has been used in endurance training is that the muscles possess large reserves of these compounds, especially glycogen. This can be proven through biochemical analysis. As the demand on the musculature increases, energy gained from the decomposition of fatty acids becomes more important.

If the athletic activity requires more energy than the maximum oxidation rate in the muscles provides, it is possible that energy may be gained through the anaerobic (without oxygen) conversion of racemic acid into lactic acid in combination with glucose. An increase in the amount of lactic acid in the muscle cells, traceable in the blood, as well as a shift in the racemic acid/lactic acid ratio (an increase in the percentage of lactic acid), is characteristic of this. This situation occurs only through intensive training, even in top racers.

Another important sign of good conditioning is the ability to postpone the buildup of these acids considerably longer than in normal individuals. Conversely, these acids can be tolerated at higher levels of concentration. This means that, despite a high percentage of acids, the muscles can still function efficiently.

The daily calorie requirement of cross-country racers is among the highest of all athletes because of the intensity of cross-country training. The average racer burns approximately 80 calories per kilo of body weight per day. This means that an average skier weighing 70 kilos needs 5,500 to 6,000 calories per day!

The need for proteins caused by the decomposition and synthesis of muscle tissue is slightly increased by cross-country

Lift lines for downhill skiing.

skiing, although clearly below that of other "strength" sports. However, under training methods of intense strength conditioning, the protein requirement can be noticeably increased.

Although the demands on the nervous system and the psyche are less obvious, they are still considerable. Unfortunately, any improvements in these areas are either difficult or impossible to measure. Observations lend to the conclusion that improvements do occur. To return to our picture of a skier gliding effortlessly along a track, we can see that there is complete unity of movement (optimum coordination), which implies a proper functioning of the nervous system. If the cross-country skier's movements are not harmonious, he cannot move smoothly and this causes him to work less efficiently—high consumption of energy sources, low speed. This is obviously not desirable for racing.

To date, it has not been possible to determine exact values or training results. Even more difficult to measure are the demands on the psyche that are doubtlessly present in cross-country skiing, specifically, and in endurance sports, in general.

There is an almost limitless array of factors that can be included in a discussion of what is the "right" or "proper" approach to competition and training. Among these we could note financial and personal independence, excellent equipment, training area, physical conditioning, and concentration. The inclusion of concentration reflects the strong psychological influences that also play a role in competitive drives during training and racing.

This creates the willpower necessary to continue in the face of exhaustion—a psychological strength. Nevertheless, even the most tenacious youth will have difficulty combating the experience of an older skier in judging the terrain, etc. It is advisable, therefore, to illustrate the limitations of a strong will that is not properly supported by physical ability and experience. Of course, a certain aggressiveness is helpful in cross-country skiing as well as in other sports, but it must be properly controlled. For example, if a skier "attacks" a fellow skier on the wrong section of the trail—exhausting himself in the process—his aggressiveness has not helped him. On the other hand, a skier must be aggressive at the start to be successful. This should illustrate the need for a proper blend of physical ability, experience, and will.

Generally speaking, it is necessary for successful athletes in endurance sports to be psychologically stable (in regard to family, occupation, finances, etc.). Frequent disruptions of interpersonal relationships have a negative effect on levels of achievement.

It is not an exaggeration to list cross-country skiing as one of the least injurious sports. Injuries such as broken legs or dislocations usually associated with downhill skiing are rare in cross-country, thanks largely to the mobility afforded the legs by the boots and bindings. "Cross-country thumbs"—a dislocation of the thumb caused by the pole straps—and dislocation of the shoulders do occur when the poles stick in the snow. It should be self-evident that head and torso injuries can arise when falling, especially on downhill runs lined with trees, rocks, or other hard objects. Bruises, broken ribs, and concussions have been known to happen. However, the risk of such injuries can be all but eliminated by a well-laid-out course. Proper use of the terrain in conjunction with the firm tracks made by machines assist even the most inexperienced skier in staying in the tracks. Of course, avoiding sharp turns and steep runs that do not have adequate runoffs can keep the risk of falling, and thereby of injuring oneself, to a minimum.

If one goes touring through untouched snow, especially at higher elevations, the risk of injury is equal to that of Alpine skiing, most specifically when storms or other unfavorable weather and snow conditions are present.

Potential damage to specific muscles owing to excessive use of one muscle group is concomitantly low. Tendon inflammations and similar disorders are not common for the same reason. When such an injury does occur, it is generally in the elbows as a result of poor pole technique or faulty poles themselves, factors that are both easy to rectify and, therefore, not worth mentioning. Further, irritations in the area of the Achilles tendon occur less in the neighboring tissue than on the heel bone proper. The appearance of such injuries is primarily the result of low-quality boots with poor heel design, in conjunction with cold temperatures. The injuries are, therefore, avoidable and not directly related to the movements of cross-country skiing.

Injuries due to low temperatures have more commonly been observed in the favorite training areas of the top Scandinavian racers, where the temperatures are between −20°C and −30°C. Weight considerations necessitate that a compromise among weight, warmth, and flexibility of clothing be reached. The increased use of synthetic materials has had a negative effect in this area. Damage to fingers, toes, nose, and ears owing to the cold has been observed. The danger of freezing, especially in a state of exhaustion resulting from intensive training, is already well known.

Although cross-country skiing itself is relatively harmless, this is not true for the dry-training periods. Running, gymnastics, weight lifting, strength/speed conditioning, and the favorite recreation of most athletes, soccer, are all well known for the injuries associated with them that are not present in cross-country skiing. These injuries include ankle sprains and dislocations from running over rough terrain; cramps and spasms in the lower back from running long distances on hard surfaces, together with a lowering of the body temperature through sweating; shin splints and other lower leg and foot disorders and sometimes even stress fractures in the bones of the middle feet traced to running long distances. Dislocated knees and tears in the ligaments and the cartilage of the knee are all common in soccer, the most often-played recreational sport of all athletes.

This period of preconditioning training for the top racers poses such enormous demands on their bodies that it is very difficult to get through this time without sustaining some sort of injury. In contrast to this, it is significant to the "harmlessness" of cross-country skiing that the injuries sustained in the spring, summer, or fall, despite the intensive training and preparation necessary during the racing season, heal completely during the winter.

The physical and psychological demands of cross-country skiing require that the athletes follow appropriate regimentation in their personal and athletic lives. The higher the level of competition, the more important this becomes. Since this is a cold-weather sport, clothing should be chosen according to its ability to maintain body heat and dispel excess moisture. This is made more difficult because of the trend toward synthetic fabrics. The forehead, ears, and hands should always be covered.

Special consideration should be given to footwear, for the summer as well as the winter. Arch supports and proper construction of the uppers—good fit and support around the heel and toes—should be sought.

As with all endurance sports, proper diet is of prime importance. Because of the high demand for calories, the menu must be well planned throughout the day. One-fourth of the total number of calories should be provided at each of the three main meals of the day, the rest to be consumed during snacks when training or racing permit. Fifty-five to 60 percent of the diet should consist of carbohydrates; approximately 18 percent, protein; and between 20 and 25 percent, fats. Snacks are helpful in making up the large amount of carbohydrates required. Because of the importance of the body's own carbohydrate reserves, these should always be well stocked. If depleted, they should be replenished at least three days before a race. During this last phase the diet should consist overwhelmingly of carbohydrates.

The mineral content of body fluids is also important in cross-country skiing. Any imbalances due to losses should be corrected. This is easily done with drinks specially prepared for racers covering distances 15 kilometers and up. Special additives are available on the market.

The demands placed on the body, especially during summer training, require intensive physiotherapeutic treatment of the muscles, tendons, and joints. Massages and trips to the sauna are excellent means of treatment.

Choosing a training program is the coach's domain. I will, however, mention a few medical observations about cross-country skiing. Unlike distance running in track and field, where athletes cover long distances at a fairly constant speed, cross-country skiing is marked by its constantly changing tempo and the corresponding changes in the demands on the body. Periods of fast tempo over flat stretches, for example, are interspersed with periods of increased anaerobic activity and even with periods of rest offered by downhill runs. This means that the body's ability to cover long distances at lower speeds will not be sufficient to bring the oxidation rate in the musculature up to the necessary levels. To do this it is necessary to work out a training program that includes excessive demands on the anaerobic processes. This can be achieved by interval running and/or hill running with occasional increases in distance or speed.

Because of the somewhat complicated movements of cross-country skiing owing to the high level of coordination required and also because of the need to increase flexibility, summer training should include exercises that imitate ski movements. Examples of this type are striding and poling on roller skis.

In determining the total health value of cross-country skiing, a distinction must be made between racing and touring, despite the obvious similarities. The changes in the body's inner organs, basal metabolism, and musculature, as a result of the physical demands on skiers pursuing higher levels of achievement, reflect an increase in ability and standards. The times are past in which an increase in the size of the heart (athlete's heart) was viewed as harmful. In a discussion of the health values of professional or high-quality sports, however, there is a problem. The sport must be viewed in its entirety, which means that the high incidence of injuries sustained during summer training must be included in the evaluation. Also, in light of new developments in preventive medicines, excessive changes in the body's makeup are not totally desirable.

Viewed in this manner, cross-country skiing as practiced "normally" appears to be an ideal sport. The constant movement for relatively long periods of time provides an excellent means of combating the sedentary lives many people now lead. It is not necessary for the heart and metabolism to increase measurably for there to be a general improvement in the body's condition. The movements have a stabilizing effect on the central nervous system and combat the many disorders in the regulation of the heart and circulatory systems common to today's sedentary life-styles. Increased energy consumption during long outings leads to a shift in the energy balance that is

Cross-country skiing promotes understanding: A German and a Norwegian discuss their equipment and know-how.

helpful in combating the most common evil of civilized man, obesity.

Before concluding, I would like to mention that cross-country skiing, with its low risk of injury or negative side effects when practiced reasonably, presents older members of our society with an excellent form of exercise. And those who complain that cross-country skiing is not a year-round sport can be encouraged to exercise a little initiative and train during the summer. If this advice is taken to heart, the sport may then be seen as year-round, with all of the advantages given to such sports by preventive medicine.

Waxing for Better Performance

The proper wax is important in all types of skiing but in cross-country it has to serve two purposes: it must allow the ski to slide across the snow in the glide phase, and it must grip the snow in the kick phase.

The problems associated with correct waxing have kept many people from trying, or in some cases continuing, cross-country skiing. They complain that waxing is similar to predicting the weather, and they point out that experts can make mistakes at both. Now, simpler waxing systems and the development of waxless skis have provided a partial answer to this problem; certainly they have done enough to help solve the problems of the casual ski tourer.

For those who wish to become more seriously involved in the sport, however, or who wish to race, there is no way to avoid learning as much as possible about waxing. Many skiers discover that not only do they get better results when they know the fundamentals, but the waxing process itself can be a challenge. A serious cross-country skier knows why he or she waxes, the relationship between the wax and the conditions on the trail, which wax to use, and how properly to apply the wax.

General Importance of Waxing

The basic element of cross-country skiing is the kick, which is used to climb and to glide. So that the kick may reach its full potential, one ski must become motionless for a split second to propel the other ski forward. To do this, you must establish firm contact between the ground and the base of the ski. This contact is brought about on waxless skis because of the special construction of the bottom. The principle is the same for various types of waxless skis: the surface of the base stands up when brushed against the grain and lies flat to allow the ski to glide.

Because the base of a wax ski is smooth, this contact must be accomplished by layers of wax. One wax must hold the ski in place during the kick phase, then release it for the glide phase. The combined characteristics of wax and snow make this shifting action work.

The Nature of Snow

To understand waxing, a brief lesson on the essential properties of snow is in order. When the temperature of water-saturated air drops below freezing—32°F or 0°C—water in the atmosphere crystallizes. That is, drops of moisture cling to various materials in the air such as dust particles and ions and, through sublimation, form ice and/or snow crystals. These crystals join together until they reach a critical weight and then they fall to earth. If they do not pass through layers of air that are above freezing, they reach the ground as snow. If they do pass through warm air, then they melt, reaching the ground as rain. The closer the temperatures of the cold air layers are to the freezing point, the larger the snowflakes become.

Falling snow and newly fallen snow, for waxing purposes, is known as new snow. Because of the dynamics of the hexagonal structure of snow crystals, the particles of new snow quickly lose their initial shape. As a result of this, only snow that has fallen within the last twenty-four hours is known as new snow. After that period it becomes known as old snow. This division of snow into two major categories with many subdivisions, such as powder snow, ice snow, and soggy or caking snow, is relatively important for purposes of competition.

It is important the skier be aware that the form and structure of individual snow particles lying on the ground are different and that they are highly sensitive to change due to wind and age; more significantly, they are affected by changes in air temperature and relative humidity. The latter of these, relative humidity, determines the general characteristics of the different types of snow. How all these factors combine determines the density of the snow.

New snow crystals (as well as powder snow crystals) are pointy, needle-shaped crystals. Because of the factors mentioned, these characteristics are quickly lost to form new shapes. Changes in the surface structure of the snow must also be noted. Frost weather combined with high relative humidity causes moisture to crystallize on the snow surface. The bladelike, sharp crystals of hoarfrost have the same characteristics as new snow crystals.

How Snow Changes

Structural changes in new snow crystals are the result of three different actions: disintegration of the new snow crystals, reconstruction of the new snow crystals, and melting.

The disintegration of new snow crystals can be divided into three categories, as follows:

Physical contact: During a snowfall the individual snow crystals may hit one another in the air or may be damaged upon contact with the earth. Once on the ground they may be further battered by the wind. In all of these instances only the nucleus survives.

Evaporation (sublimation): Over longer periods of time and temperature changes, snow crystals lying on the ground lose their shape because of a transformation from a solid to a gaseous state, without passing through a liquid phase (reverse sublimation).

In both these cases it is only the crystal's nucleus that remains unchanged. This nucleus is very small (under 2 mm in diameter) but still has a relatively jagged (sharp) structure. This type of old snow is known as *fine-grained snow.* Generally speaking, packed powder snow is included under this heading.

Melting: This subcategory could actually be seen as the beginning stage of the larger designation of melting that will be discussed shortly. As a result of warm air and direct sunlight, a transition from a solid to a liquid form occurs, known as melting. In this case the exterior of the crystal melts, leaving a small, wet nucleus with a soft, round exterior. This is also known as fine-grained snow, but with a different surface structure.

The reconstruction of new snow crystals produces the so-called wet granular snow which is commonly known for its propensity to start avalanches. This type of snow has a significant but less drastic importance to cross-country skiing. It occurs when there is a large temperature difference between the earth's surface and the surface of the snow in relation to the depth of the snow. As a result of snow's insulating ability, the temperature of the snow lying on the ground is at freezing. At the same time the earth gives off heat, causing some of the snow particles to evaporate. This moisture rises to the upper, colder layers of snow, where it refreezes, forming a frost layer within the snow layers. This frost layer consists of crater-shaped crystals with sharp, jagged edges. It occurs most often during long periods of frost in relatively shallow depths of snow, in which case the surface consists of frozen snow. If the track has been prepared by a machine, then the looser granular snow is brought to the surface. When this happens, a different wax must be used from the one suitable for the surface snow.

Melting produces wet grains of snow that quickly attach themselves to one another to form larger structures. When accompanied by above-freezing temperatures caused by the sun, warm winds, or rain, these structures combine with the other types of fine-grained and/or new snow. As a result of repetitive melting and refreezing (specifically during the night), these wet grains of snow combine to form large kernels of snow (over 2 mm in diameter). Coarse-grained snow ranging from damp to wet is known as corn snow. Frozen, dry snow is known as frozen granular snow. Frozen granular snow can include frozen corn snow, in which case it is distinguishable for its generally larger kernels and sharp contours. On the other hand, corn snow can be partially melted frozen granular snow, with rounder, softer kernels. Soggy ice snow is known as soft granular snow and finally as slush. All of these types come under the heading *coarse-grained (old) snow.*

In conclusion, of all the different forms and structures snow particles might have, it is possible to separate the particles into two major groups for the purpose of choosing a cross-country wax. These are:

- snow particles with sharp, jagged exterior structures: original new snow crystals and other fine-grained variants (with the exception of wet snow), designated as *crystalline snow*.

- snow particles with rounded, soft contours: coarse-grained snow as well as wet fine-grained and new snow. These types of snow are known as *amorphous (formless) snow*.

As mentioned previously, how these types of snow react with the cross-country waxes is dependent upon the moisture content of the snow particles. The different grades are:

Dry snow (cannot be packed in a [gloved!] hand): The drier the snow, the harder it is.

Damp snow (can be packed): The moisture present in the snow "dulls" the sharp edges of the individual particles but does not totally destroy them. It is therefore possible to have damp crystalline snow.

Wet snow (when packed it drips water): Because of the heat of the sun or warm air or rain during or following a snowfall, the individual particles lose all their sharp edges, becoming soggy, amorphous snow.

Obviously, the moisture content of snow increases drastically at temperatures over freezing. The following diagram illustrates the differences between the two types of snow on the basis of structure and moisture content.

Crystalline Snow (sharp contours)	Amorphous Snow (rounded contours)
New snow ⟍⟋ dry Fine-grained ⟋⟍ snow ⟋⟍ moist	New snow Fine-grained snow ⟍⟋ wet Coarse-grained snow ⟍⟋ damp dry

It is easier to measure the temperature of the air than that of the snow. (Generally speaking, the snow temperature is equal to the air temperature when the latter is less than freezing. Snow temperature never rises above 32°F.) As described earlier, the air temperature affects the snow both directly and—because the moisture content is related to the temperature—indirectly. Cold air does not hold much moisture (low point of saturation), and so cold air causes dry snow. The warmer the air, the more moisture it can hold; the warmer the air, the damper the snow.

Running parallel to this indirect relationship is a direct one. The hardness of the snow is directly proportional to the temperature of the air. Dropping temperatures cause the individual snow particles to contract (smaller volume than at warmer temperatures) and also harden them. (The exterior edges of the crystals shrink at cold temperatures, becoming sharper and harder.) Rising temperatures have the opposite effect, causing the individual particles to expand, becoming softer. If the temperature greatly exceeds 32°F, then the snow becomes soggy, regardless of the relative humidity.

Just as the consistency and the hardness of the individual snow particles are determined by their temperature and moisture content, the firmness of the entire snow surface is determined by its density. If the individual particles are not packed tightly on top of one another, then the snow is not dense but rather light and airy. Such snow gives under the weight of the ski. The closer the particles are to one another, the higher the density, thus providing firmer footing for the skis. A firm track has the same characteristics as hard (cold, dry) snow particles. The following is a simple summary:

- Cold air, dry snow, and a firm surface mean that the individual particles will be hard.
- Warm air, damp snow, and a loose surface mean that the individual particles will be soft.

All the previously mentioned properties of snow must be taken into consideration in choosing a wax, because different types of snow react differently to the same wax.

New snow with its sharp crystals penetrates a wax layer more easily than fine-grained old snow. Coarse-grained snow has the least penetration of all the different types of snow. Hard snow will "attack" the wax more than soft snow. We speak, therefore, of the "aggressiveness" of the snow. The finer the grain is and the harder it is, the more aggressive it is.

The Function of Wax

To provide a better understanding of the previously alluded to interaction between wax and snow, we shall go a little deeper into the two basic functions of cross-country skiing—kicking and gliding.

The Kick—Static Friction (Purchase)

In cross-country skiing, kicking with one ski sets the other ski in motion, causing it to glide. As previously described, the kick ski must remain momentarily motionless (approximately 1/10 to 1/20 of a second). For that brief moment the ski is under extreme pressure (the combined weight and strength of the body are being applied to it). This presses the (malleable) surface of the snow together under the ski without, however, covering the entire glide zones of the ski. Only those snow particles jutting above the surface of the snow come in direct contact with the glide zones. This contact causes purchase. This should clearly illustrate that the round, soft structure of amorphous snow and the sharp structure of crystalline snow will interact differently with the same wax. It should be obvious, therefore, that different waxes are needed.

Crystalline snow penetrates easily into even a hard wax, providing firm footing. Therefore, in crystalline conditions a hard wax (dry wax, canned wax) should be applied. The coarser the grain of the amorphous snow, the fewer the contact points. Amorphous snow does not penetrate the wax very well; therefore, a wax specifically designed for amorphous snow was created. To counter the snow's inability to penetrate the harder waxes, this wax has a sticky consistency. To ensure that the adhesive property of this wax is fully utilized, complete contact between the wax and the snow surface is necessary. This is made possible by the sticky, almost liquid klister waxes.

The degree of purchase differs according to the type of snow. Hard new snow (with its many hard, sharp contact points) has the highest purchase. An icy, smooth track (no direct penetration by snow particles, completely dependent upon adhesive waxes) has the lowest purchase. On an icy track there exists the danger that instead of propelling the glide ski forward the kick ski will slip backward in the track.

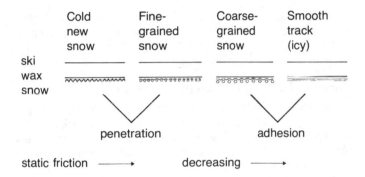

The most important factor in purchase is the number of contact points, assuming that the pressure applied to the ski is great enough to create contact between the wax layer and the surface of the snow. For this reason it is useless to kick harder if the ski is slipping backward in the kick phase. The solution is to apply a thicker layer of wax (increase penetration and/or adhesion) or to wax a larger area (increase the contact surface).

The Relationship between Kicking and Gliding

The principle of purchase is obviously useless unless seen in conjunction with the second basic function of cross-country skiing—gliding. The interaction of wax and snow should provide optimum purchase but should not have a negative effect on the glide phase.

Soft wax or even klister would provide excellent penetration and adhesion if used on hard, sharp new snow crystals. Unfortunately the contact would be so good that it would be difficult to move the ski forward. In ski jargon such a ski is said to be "dead." This means that it glides poorly at best and at worst it becomes so caked with snow that it does not glide at all.

The reverse situation would be to use too hard a wax, providing excellent gliding but little if any purchase. The wax must be matched not only to the type of snow—dry wax (crystalline snow), klister (amorphous snow)—but also to the hardness of the snow. As a rule, the wax should be as hard as possible, yet still soft enough to provide sufficient contact with the snow. The wax must always be a little softer than the snow. The shift in weight that accompanies the conversion from the kick phase to the glide phase neutralizes the penetration and/or adhesion factor.

crystalline snow = dry wax	hard snow = hard wax
amorphous snow = klister	soft snow = soft wax

Gliding—Dynamic Friction (Glide Friction)

Although an understanding of the principle of grip friction is more important for purposes of waxing—this principle determines the type of wax or waxes to be applied—dynamic friction and its dependence upon the relationship between wax and ski should also be examined.

It should be self-evident that a wax providing glide friction will have a breaking effect on the gliding properties of the ski. This is true not only in the glide phase proper but also in the change-over phase from kicking to gliding.

It is not possible to kick and glide on the same ski without a brief interlude. During this brief interlude the drag effect of those snow particles still imbedded in the wax must be eliminated. This is more difficult with the sticky klisters, to which wet snow readily adheres, than with the dry waxes (especially the harder ones). It is for this reason that synthetic skis are superior to wooden skis. The wax layer is primarily confined to the climbing zones of the ski, which are only in contact with the snow during the brief kick phase. During the glide phase the glide zones with their glide-promoting wax layer are in contact with the snow. Other advantages of synthetic skis in the glide phase will become obvious in a further discussion of the glide friction function.

We have seen how in static friction the ski comes into contact with only a portion of the snow particles on the surface of the snow. According to the laws of physics, pressure = force/surface area. Because of the small surface area under the combined force of the body's weight and strength, the resulting pressure is relatively high, creating heat. This causes the snow, which is water in a crystallized state, to melt at these contact points into minute drops of water. This has a lubricating effect, reducing friction. The formation of a water film the entire length of the ski, thereby increasing the ski's adhesive properties, is hindered by the water-repellent composition of the waxes. This is borne out by practical experience. We know that under conditions of extreme cold, the skis glide poorly—that is, they are dead, even when coated with a layer of hard wax. This happens because the lubricating layer of melted snow crystals is too thin, as a result of the intense heat given off by the relatively high pressure created.

Skis glide slower in new snow than in old, granular snow. The tiny kernels offer fewer contact points for the melting crystal to adhere to than the larger new snow crystals, thus reducing friction. Snow with a high moisture content also causes the ski to glide poorly. Such snow is very soft and malleable, coating the entire sole of the ski, causing an increase in friction. In some cases the ski's adhesive abilities (absorption) increase, creating a miniature bow wake.

However, to return to the advantages of synthetic skis, their smaller size and their separation into climbing and gliding zones are advantageous to both phases. The relatively small surface area of the gliding zones reduces the overall contact area, which in turn reduces friction. The result is similar to the principle behind ice skates. The high pressure created by the small surface area of the blades allows them to glide easily.

Properties and Types of Waxes

In order to fulfill the demands placed upon it by the glide and kick functions, the wax must possess the following characteristics:

Be wear resistant: The inner composition of wax gives it a certain elasticity (created in part by synthetic rubbers with high molecular weights). In general, the gripping ability of a waxed ski is increased by special grip waxes (base waxes, see p. 44). From all that we have said it should be obvious that aggressive snow removes the wax layer quite quickly. The length of the course also plays an important roll in this connection.

Adhere well to the ski: The sticky consistency of wax causes it to adhere to the bottom of the ski. Special application procedures for the modern polyethylene soles increase this attraction. However, despite the desire for a well-adhering, wear-resistant wax, the new synthetic waxes that go on easily also wear off easily.

Naturally the number of different waxes you use is dependent upon your knowledge of, and experience in, both the skiing and the waxing processes, as well as your willingness to become involved with the entire wax phenomenon. The earlier theoretical discussion should have illustrated that a wide range of waxes are needed to adequately cover the full gamut of track conditions. The following discussion is intended to provide the reader with the most important wax types, which are basically the same regardless of their specific brand names. Racers and other serious skiers must have a thorough understanding of all the various waxes. Accordingly, the following waxes should be included in a box of waxes:

Impregnating wax: Designed for skis with wooden bottoms, these pine tar compounds protect the ski from water and moisture. A ski that has been properly coated provides a better surface for the wax to adhere to, making it easier to wax and less susceptible to caking. This wax must be applied to new skis as well as to skis that have been stripped for cleaning purposes. It is available in liquid or spray form (easier to apply but does not last as long).

Base wax: Designed for the modern synthetic ski with polyethylene base, this wax serves to impregnate the base against moisture as well as to protect it from ultraviolet rays. Polyethylene is, of course, waterproof and wear resistant and glides easily. But even this material can be treated to enhance fully these properties. Although polyethylene appears smooth, it really has a somewhat ragged surface that picks up dust and other particles if not properly treated. Perhaps more importantly, however, untreated polyethylene will oxidize when exposed to ultraviolet rays, losing some of its glide properties. It is only in conjunction with this base wax that the optimum glide potential can be realized. It is for this reason that Alpine paraffin waxes are not suitable for cross-country.

Binder wax: These waxes are designed to help purchase waxes last longer in aggressive snow or on longer outings. They are applied over the base waxes but under the purchase wax. They are available in a can or as a spray for dry waxes, and in skare and chola for klister waxes.

Purchase wax: These waxes are color coded. The major firms generally use the same colors to represent the same wax for the dry waxes, but this is less often the case for the klisters. Because there are occasional differences, one should always

Wax and accessories: (1) dry waxes (7 types and base wax); (2) impregnating wax; (3) base wax spray; (4) wax remover spray; (5) klister in aerosol can; (6) wax box; (7) cross-country binder wax; (8) wax iron; (9) klister in tubes (in boxes); (10) thermometer; (11) spreader (cork); (12) spreader with metal spatula affixed to it; (13) scraper; (14) klister in tubes; (15) plastic spatula; (16) hand cleaner in paste form; (17) basic touring pack; (18) synthetic cleaning paper.

Waxing equipment: If necessary, the wax box can be carried in a backpack.

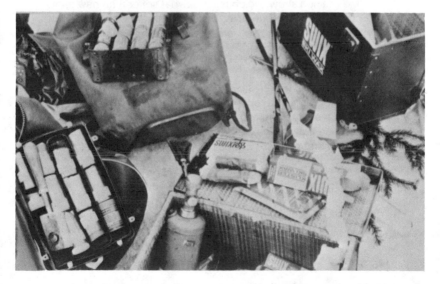

read the instructions, which are given in several languages and explain for what snow type, for what moisture content, and at what air temperature the specific color in question should be used. It is, therefore, advisable to pick one brand and become thoroughly familiar with it before branching out.

Dry wax: Also known as can waxes, these start with the hardest wax, generally light green, and run through green, blue (dark and light), violet, and red to yellow, the softest of the dry waxes. Their range of application is basically dependent upon the temperature of the air (the surface temperature of the snow generally corresponds to the air temperature).

- *Light green:* This wax is for very hard snow at very low temperatures (from about 14°F to −6°F). It is similar to the base waxes, but despite the high glide properties, it is impossible to have ideal glide conditions at extremely low temperatures.

- *Green:* Depending upon the age and type of the snow, this is for temperatures from 25°F to 14°F. For new or falling snow and higher relative humidity, blue should be used (in the climbing zone).

- *Blue:* In a typical winter climate with somewhat regular snowfall and few warming periods this is the most often used wax, for temperatures from 30°F to about 16°F, and sometimes even colder. This wax can cover all the needs of the average skier in dry new snow. Remember that old, fine-grained snow, which is somewhat softer than new snow of the same temperature, has the characteristics of snow 36°F and lower, so green should be used for old, fine-grained snow at 23°F to 14°F and for new snow at 26°F to 17°F.

- *Blue extra:* This is a special wax for 32°F to 28°F, often used by racers. It is recommended for fog and damp air, whenever blue does not grip properly. During a snowfall it is possible that the wax layer will attract moist snow particles, becoming "iced up." Blue extra is especially water repellent, hindering this buildup on the ski.

- *Violet:* For 32°F thaw, and damp snow. These so-called freezing conditions, but especially new snow, present special difficulties for waxing. The temperature and relative humidity are rarely constant over longer periods of time but rather fluctuate with the weather. This means, for example, from the time you begin waxing to the time you are finished the temperature may have risen one degree, requiring a wax fifty times softer than the one first chosen. We recommend that if the conditions appear to call for violet you first apply blue extra, and, after trying the ski and finding that it doesn't have enough purchase, then apply the violet. At almost 33°F it is occasionally necessary to rewax with red or yellow.

- *Red:* This wax is for damp, fine-grained snow from 33°F to 37°F. Its range of application is, therefore, similar to that for yellow, although yellow is generally used on new snow. Because red is not as sticky as yellow and, therefore, easier to apply, it is often used for both types of snow.

- *Yellow:* Yellow is for damp new snow. It is the softest hard wax. Because it is similar to klister in its consistency, it is sometimes called klister wax. Exercise extreme caution in applying it, because it ices or cakes up very easily (especially outside a firm track!). A sure sign that yellow should be applied is a "marble" track, caused by high relative humidity, which creates a smooth, glassy surface on the trail. For longer outings on crystalline snow at temperatures just under 32°F (blue), where there is the slightest suspicion that the temperature will rise, yellow or red should be used.

Klister: Because of the differences in structure and consistency of the various types of amorphous snow, several kinds of klister are necessary. The range of application is broader for the individual klisters than for the dry waxes. This results from the fact that the structural differences between frozen snow and wet snow are less than the corresponding differences in crystalline snow at the same temperatures. The various klisters will be presented in order of their hardness, beginning with the klister for coarse-grained snow.

- *Skare (blue klister):* This is the hardest of the klisters used at sub-freezing temperatures; it is principally for frozen snow and ice under 26°F. It is rarely used alone but rather is generally mixed with either violet or red in the middle of the ski to help provide better purchase. On hard tracks at temperatures under freezing and for longer courses it is usually applied as a base wax underneath red or silver klister.

- *Violet:* This klister has a wide range of application. It is often known as mixed snow *(wechselschnee)* klister. It is used for snow ranging from dry (also icy) to damp coarse-grained, for temperatures from 24°F to 38°F. (*Note:* This klister is sometimes marked as either red or black, depending upon the brand.)

- *Red:* The softest klister available, this is used for wet to very wet coarse-grained snow.

- *Silver:* This wax is often used by racers. It is generally applied for mixed and wet snow conditions. Its color is due to light metal additives. It is softer than violet and harder than red klister. For this reason it is especially good for wet snow in forest trails that may be strewn with pine needles or other leaves. It is often mixed with red klister to achieve better purchase.

- *Yellow:* This klister is specifically intended for damp to wet crystalline snow. Not all brands carry it, in which case, red should be used, although if available we recommend application of yellow klister. It should be used when not enough purchase is possible with yellow dry wax. It is sometimes marked as orange klister, again according to the brand.

Of course, this complete set of waxes is not necessary for the average skier. On the other hand, the use of this range of waxes can only be advantageous. However, the following basic set of waxes should be adequate for a season: *Hard waxes:* Green, blue, and red; *Klister:* Blue, violet, and red.

A few other variables must be considered in choosing what waxes to use or carry. These are:

The course layout: Does it get a lot of sun, or is it covered by shadows? Are there many steep, long uphills or long flat areas?

Elevation changes: Is the elevation at the start of the course much higher or lower than for the rest of the course? If so, there will be differences in temperature (approximately 1°F difference per 100 yards).

Number of skiers on the course: Depending on the number of skiers, the track conditions may be altered, requiring different waxes.

Season: Weather conditions change differently according to the season. In the spring, for example, the effect of the snow is much greater than in the winter.

Factors that Influence Waxing:
- Snow structure
- Air temperature
- Moisture in the air and snow
- Aggressiveness of the snow (wearing off the wax)
- Weather changes (temperature variation—precipitation)
- Personal technique and conditioning
- Length of the course
- The course layout
- Elevation changes
- Number of skiers
- Season

Waxing Accessories

Propane burner: To clean the ski; to apply base and purchase waxes.

Iron: To iron on base and purchase waxes.

Scraper: To remove excess wax after ironing on base wax. Best bet: plastic or plexiglass.

Spreader (cork or synthetic substitute): To spread (run in) hard waxes and, occasionally, klisters.

Spatula: To spread klister; to clean the ski.

Wax remover: To clean the ski, accessories, hands, and clothing. Available in liquid or spray form.

Rags: For general cleanup.

Thermometer: To measure the temperature of the air and snow. Always take readings in the open, away from cars and houses.

Wax kit: To hold waxes and accessories.

Preparation and Cleaning

It is much easier and more comfortable to wax indoors than out. It is therefore advisable to wax indoors whenever possible, but always in a waxing room. Don't burn klisters on in the hotel rooms of a ski resort. The application of the tar base as well as the cleaning of the ski is greatly facilitated by laying the ski on a flat, stable surface where the ski will not slip.

Wooden skis: Wooden skis are sometimes coated with a layer of varnish to protect them during transportation or storage.

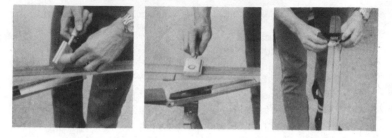

Treating polyethylene skis with base wax: melt on the wax; iron on the wax; scrape off the excess wax.

This should be removed with a fine-grain sandpaper. The ski should then be impregnated with the pine tar compound. This should be brushed on and then heated with the burner until the tar begins to bubble and is absorbed into the ski. Excess tar should be reheated and immediately wiped away. Allow to dry fully before waxing. If an aerosol base is used, spray it on evenly and allow it to dry.

Skis with tar-epoxy soles: Don't need any special coating.

Skis with polyethylene soles: Factory new soles are covered with very fine hairs that must be removed before the ski may be used. First, with wax remover, clean the sole of possible dirt and grease it might have picked up. Wait about thirty minutes until the solution has completely dried (this must be done after every application of wax remover!). Choose the appropriate wax for the conditions. Heat the iron (if possible, from between 212°F to 334°F; otherwise, set the iron to "silk"). Hold the base wax against the iron to melt the wax. Holding the iron and the wax just above the ski, drip the wax over the entire sole. If necessary, brush the wax to ensure that it is spread evenly. Then run the iron over the length of the ski to help the ski absorb the wax more thoroughly. The wax will not set properly if it is not ironed in this fashion. It is best to let these waxes harden at room temperature (not outside). Take the scraper and scrape the wax layer "down to the sole." No wax should appear to be left on the surface; actually the wax has penetrated the surface. The central groove should also be thoroughly cleaned. The glide zones of the ski are now ready to be skied upon. The climbing zone must be especially well scraped and optimally wiped quickly with cleaner. This must be done because purchase waxes will not adhere well to a ski covered with base wax residue. Base wax should be reapplied to the glide zones regularly before every race or longer outing, at the very least. The whole procedure should be repeated every two or three weeks.

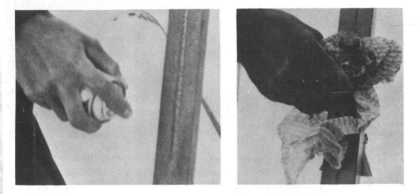

Cleaning the sole: spray on the wax remover; wipe the ski clean.

As a rule, the ski should be cleaned before every new waxing. This is a must for racing. It is also recommended if klisters are going to be used, because klisters become easily soiled with dirt and other particles that decrease the glide factor. For powder snow, especially during training, green and blue may be applied over one another.

Surface cleaning: Scrape off as much wax as possible with a spatula.

Thorough cleaning: This is done almost exclusively with a propane burner. Heat a small area of the ski with the flame and wipe the liquid wax off with a rag. Always keep the burner moving; never tarry over one spot! Wood skis will parch, and synthetic skis are especially sensitive to heat. The glue between the plies can melt, causing blisters or separation. A safer method is to use wax remover, which can be either sprayed on or applied with a rag. The remover dissolves the wax in about two minutes and can then be wiped off. Make sure that the entire ski is cleaned if it has been waxed with klister. Polyethylene soles should be cleaned with wax remover periodically and then recoated with base wax.

Waxing Your Skis

The Differences between Wooden and Synthetic Skis

Wooden skis, as well as skis with tar-epoxy soles or normal tension construction, must be "Nordically" waxed on their entire bottom surface. Synthetic skis with polyethylene soles are so constructed that it is only necessary to wax the climbing zone with hard waxes, although it is not the ski tension alone that determines where the ski must be waxed. Some ski manufacturers mark those areas of the ski that must be waxed. If this is not the case, it is possible to determine where the ski should be waxed by holding the two skis sole to sole and lightly pressing them together. Where the skis do not touch in the center is the area that must be waxed. This area is usually 2½ feet (80 cm) long, centered around the front of the bindings. This full length should be waxed for cold, hard snow (cold dry wax, skare). Softer waxes (specifically klisters) should be applied on a length of 2 feet (60 cm) or so. In this case, no klister should be applied behind the boot heels.

A Few General Rules

There are major differences in the conditions that call for klisters and those that call for dry waxes. However there are a few basic rules that should be followed regardless of which wax is to be applied. These are:

- The ski must be clean and dry before the wax can be applied.

- A thicker and/or longer layer of wax provides better climbing. If the ski does not have enough purchase, more of the same wax should first be applied before changing waxes. If the skis in question are synthetic, the wax layer should be extended forward, so that the ball of the foot can apply greater pressure (primarily for climbing). If this does not provide the desired purchase, a softer wax may be applied over the existing layer of harder wax. A harder wax, however, should never be applied over a softer layer. If the initial wax is too soft, it must be removed before a harder wax may be applied.

- Under normal circumstances no more than two wax layers (not counting the base wax) should be applied on top of one another (dry waxes—e.g., green and blue) or mixed with one another (klister—e.g., red and silver).

- Polyethylene soles should always be coated initially with a thin layer of heated wax: ironed-on dry wax or heated klister. The use of heat helps the wax adhere to the ski.

- A thin layer should be applied for new snow.

- The direction in which the wax is applied and spread has no bearing on its effectiveness.

Waxing with dry wax: rub on the wax; spread the wax with a cork.

Dry Waxes (Green to Violet)

Tear the foil that covers the can approximately ¼ inch down from the top. In some brands the wax may be pushed up from the bottom to expose the surface.

Apply the wax by rubbing it onto the ski with short strokes of the hand, as evenly as possible over the entire area of the ski to be waxed. The central groove should be waxed with a very thin layer of wax. If more than one type of wax is to be applied, only the hardest should be applied to the groove. The first wax layer should be ironed on if you are waxing synthetic skis. Ironing on wax is also advantageous for wooden skis. Allow the ironed-on layer to cool. If the wax was ironed on indoors, go outside!

Polish this ironed-on layer with a cork (and only with a cork!) to a smooth surface.

Apply at least one more thin layer of wax and polish it with the cork. For longer courses several additional thin layers should be applied and corked. These additional layers should not be heated unless absolutely necessary; in no case should the last layer be heated. The softer the snow (temperature, moisture!), the thicker the layer.

If the ski is waxed with two different hard waxes (e.g., blue and blue extra), they should become mixed at the edges. First apply the harder wax with an iron; then rub the second layer into the first with a cork. This is generally necessary at temperatures in and around 32°F.

The lower the temperature, the longer the area waxed should be—thus, for instance, light green may be applied the length of the ski.

Dry Waxes—Klister Wax (Yellow)

Because of the consistency of yellow (and sometimes red), a different method of application must be followed. These waxes must not be applied by rubbing the can of wax directly on the ski! The can should be lightly squeezed so that the wax comes out a little bit at a time and can then be dabbed onto the ski. Twist the can to tear the sticky strands as you pull it away from the ski. Set a cork aside for use on yellow so that the next time you want to wax with green it won't have yellow mixed in with it! Better yet, heat yellow and iron it on. If the yellow sticks too much, it is possible to apply a thin layer of blue over it. Let the yellow harden (preferably outside), so that it is easier to rub the blue over it. If possible, heat the blue a little before applying it. This is an exception to the rule that a harder wax should not be applied over a softer one, although the end effect in this case is a mixture, which should be ironed together if possible.

Binder Wax for Dry Waxes

Binder wax comes in two forms: as a spray or in a can (like dry waxes). The spray is faster and easier to apply (spray evenly in a thin layer and allow to dry), but it is not as effective. Because of its consistency it should be dabbed out of the can much as yellow is spread evenly with an iron; if the wax is not heated, it will clump up on the cork. Heating has the further advantage on polyethylene soles of forcing the wax deeper into the pores of the ski. This counters the glide—dampening properties of the binder wax if it is left on the surface. Wipe away any excess

Applying klister from a tube: the skier (Georg Zipfel) clearly illustrates how far in front of and behind the binding the wax should be applied.

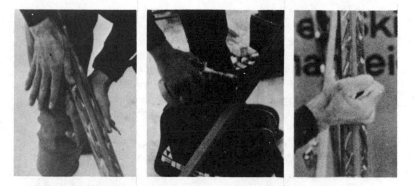

Applying klister: spread the klister with the thumb; apply the wax with the aid of a propane burner; mix two klisters—first red, then silver.

binder with a rag. If possible, iron on the binder and allow it to harden outside.

The usual dry waxes (light green, green, or blue) should be applied outside and without heat in several thin layers as described earlier. If the dry wax were heated, it would mix with the binder and hinder the gliding potential of the ski. The dry waxes should, therefore, be carefully applied so as not to mix with the binder.

Generally speaking, binder-and-dry-wax skiing is done under granular snow conditions: a hard crust next to the track and corn snow on the track. This wax combination may also be used on a frozen snow track at low temperatures (light hoarfrost buildup—crystalline surface) with better results than those achieved with klister. At temperatures near 32°F and high relative humidity, klister (skare) may be applied between the binder and the dry wax layers.

Klister (Skare)

Klisters change in consistency, depending upon the temperature. This wax becomes hard as rock at cold temperatures and gooey at warm temperatures. For this reason, only those klisters for temperatures around 32°F (red, silver, and yellow) can be applied without heat. It is almost impossible to squeeze violet and skare out of the tube without heat. If possible, you should wax at room temperature. If this is not possible, then the klister tube should be heated with a burner before the wax is applied. If the klister hardens, reheat the tube. Squeeze the tube evenly with the fingers and spread the klister evenly down both sides of the center groove in long straight strokes, in short diagonal strokes, or by dabbing it on, always at a constant thickness. If necessary, the hardening klister may be lightly warmed on the ski and immediately spread. Use either the spatula or the heel of your hand for this purpose. Do not apply any wax directly to the groove but rather spread the wax layers on either side of it, into it. If it is very cold or you have little time, heat the klister and rub it in with a cork.

Wood skis should have one thin layer of wax; polyethylene skis should have two layers, the first of which should be applied hot (to help the wax adhere to the ski).

The thickness of the klister layer is very important! Klister should be applied in a thin layer for wet snow, especially for wet new snow. For a colder, harder track or for longer outings, a thicker layer should be applied.

Because damp and wet coarse-grained snow can have so many variables, it is quite common to mix klisters (usually two), for instance, red and violet, red and silver, red and yellow, or silver and violet. Experienced waxers can correctly analyze the track and mix the right klisters together. To mix klisters, apply first one and then the other next to each other on the ski and then rub them into the ski. For an icy, very large-grained, hard track, skare can be used alone, over the entire length of the ski if necessary (see light green) to increase the wax's grip on the ski and on the snow without decreasing the glide. Normally a dab of violet is mixed in with the skare to provide better purchase, or sometimes an entire layer of violet is applied over the skare. Skare can also be used as a base wax for other klisters, extending the life of the klisters.

A well-waxed klister ski should provide good purchase without sticking during the glide phase. Klister tends to ice up under changing conditions, such as coarse-grained snow ranging from damp to dry and fine-grained snow lying in the shadows. We recommend a thin layer of dry wax (usually blue) to cover up the klister. This should be applied by first letting the klister harden, applying blue onto the frozen klister, and then rubbing it in carefully. If it is not cold out, the dry wax must first be heated and then ironed on.

Waxing For Races

If possible, check the snow conditions and the temperature changes a day or two before the race. Likewise, if possible, try out the track with different waxes to find the best combination.

As a cardinal rule, always let the skis cool outside before testing them. Ski for at least ten minutes before coming to any decisions about waxing. Most waxes must be broken in before they will exhibit their true qualities. This method is the only way to test the wax—not faith or suspicion. After this short test, two or three possibilities should surface, all of which must be further tested before deciding. Luck or chance should not have the final say.

If weather conditions are holding stable and the snow is cold snow, either crystalline or amorphous, a pair of skis can be waxed the day before. If the conditions remain constant, these skis will glide better than newly waxed skis. It is better to use a harder wax in this case, as it is always possible to add a softer wax to provide more purchase.

On the day of the race the temperature should be observed for a couple of hours before the start of the race to see what effects it will have on the track during the race. If the conditions are

His choice of wax was completely wrong.

unstable, and if it is possible, wax one pair of skis and test them out, and set a second pair aside with everything but purchase wax on them. If the waxed skis turn out to be totally wrong, the other pair may be quickly waxed and used. Do not test the skis around the starting line. The snow there is warmer because of the number of people on it and it is also dirty, which can foul up a klister-waxed ski.

The ideal mass start: wide starting area, many tracks.

Cross-Country Ski Technique

In sports, the word *technique* is used to describe how a specific task can be completed effectively and economically. This means the technique must not only make a specific sport possible, but must also cause it to be performed with the least expenditure of energy and strength to ensure a high standard of performance.

Because of differences in terrain and track conditions, several techniques are needed in cross-country skiing. These are divided into two categories: running and downhill forms.

Seen in their totality, the possible forms are the same for a ski tourer and a racer. Every individual style of the running form (sometimes, although not always correctly, referred to as the stride type) possesses the basic technical elements needed for cross-country skiing. The differences are naturally the result of differences in the capabilities and conditioning of the individual skier. Tourers practice the *base* forms of running technique, whereas racers exhibit the *end* forms.

The reasons for this division are found in the different levels of athletic talent, motor skills, experience, and physical condition of the skiers. The end forms are characterized by stronger, quicker movements.

It is possible that a skier who, to the layperson looks relatively good and appears to be fast and strong, may well have achieved the end form of a technique such as diagonal stride, although only in a rough way (such as by using false planting of the poles or excessive swinging of the arms). On the other hand, a skier who is neither strong nor in great condition may not be able to ski great distances but may have good coordination and, therefore, may have fully mastered a base form of running technique.

Every skier who is able to propel himself forward will be fulfilling the principle of purpose. As he begins to move a bit more economically, his technique will become better, "cleaner." It is on this basis—the same technique form for everyone, beginners and racers alike, differentiated only by proficiency—that the following material on technique is offered.

Diagonal Striding

The diagonal stride is the most commonly used technique under normal conditions. It can be used on flat lands as well as inclines. Most skiers use this technique when they are in heavy snow and, when they are tired, sometimes even on slight dips. The basic technique of diagonal striding plays an important role in other forms as well, such as double poling with a step, pendulum step, bow step, or even herringbone step.

Proper diagonal striding is a relatively complex coordination of constantly shifting individual movements of the arms and legs.

1: Normal walking.

2: Walking on skis without poles.

Because of this we go into it in greater detail than we do for the other techniques. Diagonal striding is basically a more advanced form of normal walking on skis in conjunction with poles. Let's consider both the base and end forms.

Base form: The natural rhythm of walking is that when one leg is behind the other, the opposite hand is also held back. At the same time that the other leg is swung forward, the opposing hand moves forward.

This movement is also typical of cross-country skiing. When one ski is pushed forward the opposite hand is also swung forward. If you are using poles, the kick of one ski is assisted by your planting the opposite pole. This is the base form of the diagonal stride.

3: Basic form of diagonal striding (woman open-meet skier).

4: Basic form (Peter Zipfel, "out walking").

End form: The end form is characterized by a dynamic show of strength reflected in fuller movements which allow the skier to cover more ground. In the following series of photographs the end form is shown in its ideal state, with perfect coordination of all movements. In this section only the form is illustrated. In the next section the reasons why these specific movements are desired will be explained in biomechanical terms.

The diagonal stride is often referred to as a cyclical style of movement. This means that the same movements are constantly being repeated.

The Phases of Diagonal Striding:
- pre-kick phase
- kick phase
- swing phase
- glide phase
- arm/pole action
- push with the arms
- swing of the arms

Although the individual motions of the technique do not function separately, they are singled out for purposes of instruction. Let's examine the complete motion, created by coordinated leg movements.

5: Diagonal lines show coordination: right foot/left hand; left foot/right hand.

Leg Work

PREPARING FOR THE KICK

In photo 6/3 the skier is gliding on his left leg, while his right leg is gliding forward. The left knee is somewhat flexed (the lower part of the leg is perpendicular to the ski). This positioning of the left leg remains constant as the right leg is pushed further forward (compare the mirror image of the motion, shown in 6/8), although the upper body begins to lean forward slightly.

In 6/4 the legs are parallel to one another. This means that the left leg is now ready to enter the kick phase. Notice the sharp bends of the ankle, knee, and waist and the positioning of the upper body. As a result of this coordination, the body's center of gravity, located in the hip region, is pushed forward over the toes. This means that the kick will force the body's center of gravity rapidly forward. This stage of the pre-kick phase is also known as the *gravity shift*.

The differences between the end form and the base form at this stage are clearly visible (see 3/3 and 4/4). Notice how the three joints (ankle, knee, and waist) are not as flexed and that the body's center of gravity is back over the center of the feet.

KICK PHASE

The kick phase begins immediately after the gravity shift with the lifting of the heel (6/12). The left leg is then "exploded" downward onto the snow under constant pressure from the ankle, knee, and hip. In 6/5, directly before the kick ends, the knee is still slightly flexed. Although 6/1 is a mirror image showing the right leg, it does illustrate the almost full extension of the kicking leg whereby the ski is held flat on the snow by the pressure exerted by the toes. That ends the kick phase. The kicking leg and the torso should create a relatively straight line.

6: End form of diagonal striding (Georg Zipfel).

A comparison with the base form shows that the kicking leg is not as fully extended (4/2, but even better in 3/4). In these cases there is little pressure exerted onto the snow, so that the center of the ski lifts slightly. The kick is ended too early.

SWING PHASE

After the kick, as a result of the contracting muscles, the left leg completes its backward motion. The end of the ski will thus

be lifted up from the snow (see 6/10 and then 6/6). Then it begins to swing forward (6/7). The ski should be set automatically back onto the snow without any additional body movements, approximately in the middle of the swing (6/8). The earlier method of setting the ski back down onto the track only after the legs were once again parallel is rarely practiced today. However at this point the ski should be under the weight of the leg, but with no additional body weight. The latter is not added until the end of the forward swing, at which point the two legs should be parallel.

The swing phase then consists of a back swing, which is relaxed with little stress, and then a stressed forward swing of the leg.

GLIDE PHASE

After setting the left "swing" leg onto the track, a slight weight shift onto this leg begins. This shift increases as the right leg begins its kick phase (6/9) and is completed when the right leg finishes its kick (6/10).

From that moment all of the body weight is on the left "glide" leg, until the shift to the other leg begins (6/11). For one brief moment there is a total glide—a glide without the kicking ski or the poles being in contact with the ground (from 6/10 on; 6/6 also shows a later stage).

The positioning of the knee is very important in the "glide" leg. It should be well bent at the beginning of the kick (6/9) and at the end of the other leg's kick (6/5 and 6/1). At the end of the kick, during the swing phase of the other leg, the "glide" knee should become increasingly bent (6/6 and 6/7) until at the end of the swing phase the lower leg becomes perpendicular to the ski (shown here on a slight incline, 6/11). This form, which is typical of present racing technique, will be further discussed in the next section. Until recently it was common practice to teach skiers to bend the "glide" knee during the whole phase to such a degree that the lower leg and the ski formed an angle of 90° or less.

Arm/Pole Action

PUSH WITH THE ARMS

Photo 6/1 shows the position of the pole and arm at the end of the forward swing of the right arm. At this point the right leg should be outstretched in the opposite direction. As the right leg completes its backward swing, the right arm should be completing its forward swing (6/10). Photo 6/6 captures the simultaneous completion of the return motion of the (left) "swing" leg and the forward swing of the (left) arm. The start of the right leg's forward swing should be fully synchronized with the planting of the right pole (6/2). The pole should be placed next to the (left) "glide" leg, planted at an angle of approximately 70°, opening frontward.

As soon as the pole has been planted, the right arm should apply pressure to it (a slight bowing of the pole resulting from this pressure is clearly illustrated in 6/2). Bending the elbow increases the pressure brought to bear on the pole (6/11 and then 6/3), allowing the hand to drive the pole in as quickly as possible (6/4 and 6/5). The acute angle thereby created between the pole and the ground increases the net effect of poling. In 6/5 (the right arm is somewhat extended; the hand is low) the arm is just behind the body and the poling motion is almost over. (Seen from behind, the pole and the arm should form an obtuse angle.) A moment later (not shown) the rear motion of the (right) arm is completed. The arm and pole should form a straight line (approximately 180°, sometimes even more).

BACK AND FORWARD SWING OF THE ARMS

The push on the poles lasts a very short time (approximately 0.06 seconds), finishing before the kick of the opposing leg. Photo 6/1 illustrates how the pole tips leave the snow and how the arm and pole begin to swing backward at the moment the leg completes the kick phase. To allow the arm to swing freely and in a relaxed fashion, the hand begins to loosen its grip on the pole. In 6/6 the end of the back swing of the right pole corresponds exactly to the beginning of the left leg and arm

7: Diagonal striding—opening the hand (Peter Zipfel).

forward swing. At the moment of pure glide (only the musculature of the right "glide" leg is tensed; the muscles of the left leg and both arms are at their most relaxed stage) the skier is in his most extended position. The left hand and the tip of the right pole are fully separated. The hand is fully open; the pole supposedly hangs between the thumb and the forefinger (6/6 or, even better, 7). The right arm swings loosely; the elbow is slightly bent (6/7 to 6/10). Then the hand tightens its grasp on the pole once again (6/7). This causes the tip of the pole to remain low during the forward swing, rising above the handle only briefly (6/8). In 6/10 the forward swing and, therefore, one cycle of the right arm have been completed. The tip of the pole is barely clearing the ground; the hand is a little higher than the shoulder.

During the entire arm cycle, the arm is always held parallel to the ski without any lateral movement.

The Fundamentals of Movement

In this section, which is almost scientific in detail, are a few explanations concerning the exact movements of the diagonal stride. This will perhaps clarify a few elements of motion for interested skiers or racers, and enable them to use such information to their own benefit.

The values given in this section (of angles and for strength and time measurements, among others) are taken in part from the book *Skisport,* which is the collected work of several Soviet authors. Values were also used from two biomechanical experiments based on films taken at international competitions (see the bibliography, under Novosad and Waser, for further information).

To illustrate some of the findings, we use two series of photographs that can be easily compared (from the International Glocknerlauf race, 1976).

First a few interesting figures are quoted related to the diagonal-stride cycle (two individual steps) on a level track, as performed by good skiers under different glide conditions. The distance covered by one cycle varied between 3.5 and 6.5 meters. The time required was between 0.3 and 1.5 seconds. At this rate a skier would ski between 40 and 75 cycles per minute. This corresponds to an average speed of 4 to 6.4 meters per second (about 14–23 kilometers/hour or 8.4–13.3 miles/hour)!

A glance at photo series 8 and 9 shows that skier Arto Koivisto (K) needed approximately 1.5 seconds (at four photos per second) for one full cycle (9/1 to 9/6) in heavy snow (end of May, wet new snow on a base of jelly snow [*sulzschnee*] at a height of 2,200 meters). The tempo of an average "open" racer (O) is not much slower (in 8/1 his right leg is already further forward, closer to the left leg than K's; in 8/6 O's right leg is starting its kick, while K's right leg has already completed its back swing!).

Pre-Kick Phase

The results of Novosad's experiments provide us with measurements of the angles formed by the various joints during individual phases of diagonal striding. A comparison of the measurements for the top ten finishers and the last ten finishers shows that there is little difference between the two, at best no more than within the groups themselves. Variations in the execution of the diagonal-stride technique owing to personal style appeared to play a far less important role than conditioning. Nevertheless, especially large differences between the averages of the better and the poorer group for certain measurements were noted. Photo series 8 and 9 are intended to illustrate what is considered good or poor during the individual phases of diagonal striding. The following average positions are based on the gravity-shift point.

The diagrams show how the better skiers coordinate their movements more fully, bend forward more, and are generally tighter in their technique. A crucial point here is the almost identical angle formed between the lower legs and the ground and between the thighs and the upper body. The angle formed by the latter is greater than that of the former (8° difference). Even if the body's center of gravity is somewhat falsely placed in the middle of the body for purposes of simplicity, it is still much further forward in a good skier (see Diag. 1).

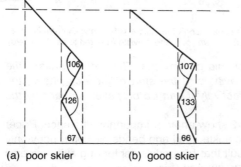

(a) poor skier   (b) good skier

Diag. 1. Comparison of body angles in good and poor skiers.

8, 9: Diagonal striding—a comparison of techniques. *Top row:* Open-meet skier (referred to as "O" in text); *bottom row:* Arto Koivisto (referred to as "K" in text).

The advantage should be obvious: *The further forward the body's center of gravity is at the start of the kick phase, the faster and more effectively it can be propelled forward by the kick.*

Photos 8/2 and 9/2 show another important difference. Racer O does not bend his ankle at all and bends his upper body only slightly, with the result that his body's center of gravity remains behind his supporting surface (foot).

A comparison with the preceding pictures (8/1 and 9/1, respectively) clearly illustrates that the angles formed by O's body remain almost unchanged, while K goes directly from perpendicular lower legs and an upright upper body to a strong flexing of the ankle and hips. This quick downward shift creates a short-lived weightlessness followed by stronger pressure (similar to the downward shift in weight of Alpine skiing). Actually the shift in weight is the difference between 50 percent and 100 percent of the body's weight bearing on the ski. The strong flexing of the three joints stretches the respective extensor musculature (the thighs, front, and back for the hips and knees, the calves for the lower legs), preparing them for the next phase. The muscles can then contract with greater force. In addition to this, the back swing increases the distance of the acceleration movement forward. The calf muscles are especially important in the motion, as they lift the foot from the ground. This means that if the body's center of gravity is shifted far forward in the gravity shift, it can provide an effective counterweight to the kicking action, which allows for a faster, stronger, more explosive kick phase.

Kicking

As shown in 6/12, the kick phase actually begins by applying pressure with the heel. According to Novosad's angle measurements, the body's center of gravity should be well forward at this stage. The average angle formed by the glide and kick legs was found to be 7° smaller in the good group than in the poor group. This means, once again, that the actual kick-stretch movement is begun much earlier!

This is further supported by 8/6 and 9/5. The larger opening of racer O's legs is due only partly to a later kick phase. O is guilty of a number of rather typical mistakes made by inexperienced skiers—for example, his left leg is too far forward (note the positioning of the calf—it forms an angle greater than 90°, (whereas, in 9/5, K forms an angle of less than 90°). This means that O's weight is on his left leg as he is gliding forward.

This causes two significant disadvantages. His kick is not coordinated with his center of gravity, and he cannot utilize his body weight effectively in conjunction with expanding his muscles. The vertical pressure exerted (see diag. 2/1 and 2/4), supplemented by the proper purchase wax, will be minimal. This is why many skiers who start their kicks too late complain that their skis are too slippery! In addition, because of the late start of his kick phase—his right leg is already extended—O will be unable to utilize his kick to its fullest. Not only does the amount of pressure created remain small, but the overall strength of the kick is also held at a minimum. Impulse = Mass (strength) × Speed (distance divided by time).

Good skiers, on the other hand, can create enough pressure through the kick (vertical pressure) to equal twice the weight of the body.

Forward movement, however, is dependent upon more

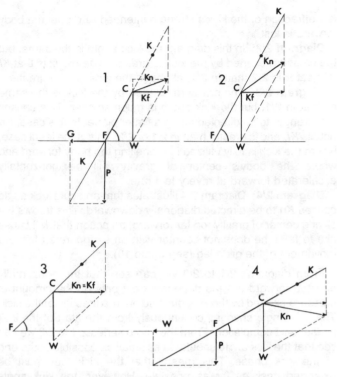

Diag. 2. Direction and amount of pressure exerted in kick phase.

C = Center of gravity   F = foot
W = Body weight   K = Kick force
G = Glide component (horizontal)   Kn = Net kick
P = Pressure component (vertical)   Kf = Forward horizontal drive

variables than the amount of vertical pressure exerted. The downward and backward pressure created by the extended muscles is actually used for the reverse action it creates. As illustrated in the strength parallelogram, this pressure is directed vertically upward and horizontally forward. The amount of the forward pressure is dependent upon the amount of pressure exerted by the kick and the size of the kick angle.

The two opposing forces that must be neutralized during the kick are the body weight W (gravitational force) and the kick strength of the legs.

Diagram 2/1: The net value of the kick (Kn) computed from K and W is directed diagonally upward. The actual forward drive (Kf) is shown in another parallelogram with Kn. Kf is less than

Kn; a fraction of the kick's strength intended to propel the body forward is lost.

Diagram 2/2: In this diagram the kick angle is the same, but the pressure exerted by the kick is greater. The result is that *Kf* is greater in 2/2 than in 2/1, although the loss is also greater.

Diagram 2/3: The pressure exerted by the kick is the same as that in 2/1, but the kick angle is much smaller. This causes the strength to be directed along a flatter plane. In this case, *Kn* equals *Kf,* and is greater than in 2/1 or 2/2. This is the ideal case, where the kick is fully utilized in propelling the body forward and where the body's center of gravity will be horizontally accelerated forward at a very fast rate.

Diagram 2/4: Diagram 2/4 illustrates that an acute kick angle causes *Kn* to be directed diagonally downward. This throws the skier's center of gravity too far forward, an action that will cause him to fall if he does not counter with an exaggerated forward movement of the glide leg (see photo 10).

From diagrams 2/1 to 2/3 we can see that the horizontally directed forward drive is dependent not only on the amount of pressure exerted by the kick but also on the direction of the kick. The kick angle changes continuously from the start of the kick phase to its completion. From the photo series 2/1 to 2/3 we can see that the kick angle should be as small as possible at the end of the kick phase. This means that the kick foot must be extended back as far as possible. However, the kick angle

10: Diagonal striding—glide phase (open-meet skiers).

cannot be held too long in this position; to do so would have the negative effects illustrated in diagram 2/4.

If the kick angle becomes too acute, it causes the body's center of gravity to drop still further and shift to the rear. The full weight of the body would fall on the kick leg, stopping it from swinging back and forth. The entire strength of the kick would be lost. A forward shift of the body's center of gravity is not possible without an uneconomical expenditure of energy.

In addition, the level action of the thighs of the glide leg would be overtaxed. Most importantly, though, it would be impossible to ski very long. The purchase of the ski (friction × pressure) would not be sufficient. The low pressure would cause the ski to slip in the track. Diagrams 2/1 and 2/4 show that the glide component of the kick to the ground is low if the kick angle is large, but that the pressure component is high (diag. 2/1). If the kick angle is acute, then the glide component will greatly exceed the pressure component.

Lastly, if the kick angle is too acute, the kick's power cannot be increased throughout the kick phase. On the contrary, maximum power is possible during only two-thirds of the kick phase, after which the power curve drops until it reaches zero at the beginning of the back swing.

These theoretical considerations correspond fully to practical considerations. According to Novosad's angle tabulations, the last kick angle recorded for the faster group (Group I) was only 2° smaller than that for the slower group (Group II). However, the lower-leg angle for Group I was 6° smaller, the ankle was flexed more, and the thigh was more upright. This means, once again, that the body's center of gravity is forward, so that it can be whipped forward faster with the same kick angle.

Modern waxing techniques have increased the tendency to end the kick at an earlier stage. The short climbing zones (see page 52) require that the pressure component be directed vertically downward to provide optimum purchase. In 1970 the average kick angle of the test skiers was around 45°. This had increased to approximately 53° by the end of 1974.

Conclusion: The kick should be begun as soon as possible with an immediate, hard explosive action. The emphasis is no longer on the rear extension of the leg outward, but rather on the pressure extended downward to the ground. This means that the kick can be ended earlier (visually observable by the shorter stride and more erect posture), still allowing for a high-power impulse.

Swing Phase

The relaxed back swing of the leg allows the heavily strained kick muscles to recover. The front flexor muscles of the hip joints are thus expanded so that they can snap forward quickly for the forward swing that follows.

The leg cannot rely solely on gravity to swing it forward. It must be actively and dynamically swung forward. The swinging leg contributes greatly to the whole drive. The power of the swing is assisted by the braking action of the swinging leg when it comes within about 7½ inches of the glide leg (see 6/8 and 9/4). The more suddenly this occurs, the more powerful is the swing, creating a forward-moving inertia (similar to the forward movement of car passengers when the car stops short).

It is possible to distinguish between two types of forward swing. Many skiers emphasize a forward swing of the hips and upper thighs. This causes a slight flexing of the knee, which makes the calf hang. Power is lost through the braking action. Other skiers concentrate on sliding the calves forward. The knee remains relatively extended (see 9/1 and 9/4), and the "lever" of the leg is longer and stiffer, increasing the power. This inertia can increase the pressure five to seven times. This corresponds to approximately one-fifth or one-sixth of the horizontal power of the kick! Photos 8 and 9 prove useful in this respect also. We see that racer O does not execute a relaxed back swing nor does he have an active forward swing (8/3 illustrates the turning point of the left leg). The leg drops to the snow with a thud at the end of the kick (causing more friction and drag!) and, because of the flexed knee, the leg is shoved forward as opposed to being swung forward (8/4). A comparison of the first two pictures of both series clearly illustrates that O needs much more time to bring his right leg forward for the gravity shift than K does.

The modern running technique, with its dynamic execution and high tempo, increases the alternation of tensing and relaxing the muscles and also increases the drive produced by the swing phase.

Glide Phase

The swing phase of the opposite leg is closely coordinated with the glide phase, which occurs almost simultaneously. If the swing leg is not actively swung forward after the kick, as a result of an improper shifting of the body's weight (and is, therefore, shoved over the snow under the burden of the body's weight), then it creates drag on the ski, slowing the glide of the front ski.

Note: Full utilization of the kick and the swing is only possible with proper one-leg gliding! The longer the swing phase lasts, the slower the speed of the glide phase is!

The importance of flexing the knee and the resulting positioning of the calf was previously discussed on page 76. Present-day racing technique calls for the knee to be straightened somewhat at the end of the glide phase, an action that forces the calf forward, sometimes until it becomes perpendicular to the ground (see photos 9/7 and 9/4; 11 and 12).

11, 12: Glide phase—positioning of the calf (Arto Koivisto).

This creates the following advantages:

- Straightening the glide leg lifts the hips, allowing for free, effective forward swing of the swing leg. If the hips are too low, the knee of the swing leg must be bent too severely, and the body weight will not be applied to the ski early enough, thus losing impulse.
- Straightening the glide leg also increases the tension span, and thereby also increasing the effectiveness of the gravity shift that follows, by acting as a counterweight.
- The body's center of gravity is shifted forward as a result of the increased lean in the upper torso. This counterbalances any vertically directed swing caused by following through with the glide leg (photos 11 and 12).
- The additional forward push of the calf is aided by the simultaneous start of the opposite arm's poling action. This

lengthens the glide phase. The body's center of gravity, despite its general shift forward, remains briefly behind the glide foot. This acts as a power reserve and can greatly increase the glide potential of the ski.

- At the same time, the relatively rigid forward and down propulsion of the glide leg provides a firmer base for the poles, whose pressure is directed backward. The pressure created by poling is used more effectively in this case than if the knee were bent to a greater degree.

The forward push of the calf during the extension of the glide knee is only logical if you use a one-legged glide technique, and then only in the second stage of the glide phase (when the opposite leg has completed its kick). This must not be confused with the "escape" step, which is a forward push of the calf during the kick to maintain balance. Photos 8/3 through 8/6 clearly illustrate the constant positioning of the forward calf, whereas photos 11 and 12 portray the changing positions. Photo 13 illustrates the escape step even more clearly, with the rear leg creating more drag than drive.

The measurements of the glide phases of the top racers prove their superiority over the slower racers. The glide time (measured as a percentage of the time needed for one full stride), as well as the distance covered per stride, is greater than are the equivalent measurements for the poorer skiers.

13: Glide phase — "escape step" (woman open-meet skier).

Arm/Pole Action

Along with the kick and forward swing of the leg, the third means of propelling yourself forward in diagonal striding is the arms. Their effectiveness is dependent upon good coordination with the legs in terms of the timing, positioning, and strength of their movements. This means that the arms must be at the right place, at the right time, with the proper strength or lack of strength.

This coordination is illustrated as it should be executed in photo series 6 (as well as series 9) and is explained beginning on page 66. The ideal execution   (a simultaneous planting of the poles with the start of the leg's forward swing; end of the pole action just before the start of the kick) holds for normal glide conditions (level, good snow). If the glide conditions are not good, then the coordination must be altered slightly (see diagonal striding uphill, p. 81).

Perfect coordination of the arms and legs is the primary mark of a technically good skier. A technically poor skier is easily identifiable by improper coordination of the arms and legs. Series 8 and 9 prove this. Racer O's poor arm coordination strikes the reader immediately: his arms are always ahead of his legs in their movements. In 8/2, racer O has ended both his right-pole motion and the forward swing of his left arm at the same time that he has just completed his gravity shift. Looking at K, we see that both arms are still in the middle of their motions. If O were to plant his pole normally, immediately following the forward swing (see K, 9/3), his left arm and leg would be working in a parallel fashion as opposed to a diagonal one. This would be a totally unnatural movement (except for ambling horses—humans do not amble). In order to avoid this mistake, O instinctively holds his pole in the air as a means of compensation but still plants it too early. The pole is planted in 8/3 as the left leg reaches its turning point. Actually (by chance), 8/6 shows how the pole is swung forward to try to compensate for the poor coordination. A comparison between 8/4 and 9/4 shows that in this case his coordination is all right. But 8/5 shows that his pole push ends just before the gravity shift and that his right pole is further forward than K's. K's leg movements are further along in their respective phases at this point also (right kick leg). In 8/6, O's legs correspond to K's in 9/5—with both of O's arms flailing uselessly in the air.

We have described these mistakes in detail because they represent more than a question of aesthetics. The photography shows that although O's total active push phase is of the same direction as K's, K's poling and kicking complement one another; O's do not. Additionally, 8/1 and 8/3 show that the tips of O's poles have not properly penetrated the snow surface. O exerts very little pressure on his poles, creating little forward drive. Because of his poor coordination, O must hold his pole above the ground at the end of the forward swing. This means that his arm cannot relax at all.

Effective poling is of the utmost importance. In modern racing, it is gaining more and more significance. Of course the prerequisites for good coordination do not appear to be all that favorable. The muscles of the arms are much weaker than the leg muscles. The average vertical pressure exerted by the arms is about one-tenth that achieved by the legs. In addition to this, the pressure exerted by the arms on the poles is created by a rather inefficient system of leverage. This inefficiency is due to the length of the arm and the flexibility of the elbow, which works as a lever on the body's center of gravity.

There are, however, certain advantages. The sharp tips cause no friction with the snow. This means that the angle formed by the pole and the ground can be sharper than the kick angle. This increases the net horizontal drive (to approximately one-fifth of the pressure exerted by the kick, so that the efficiency coefficient is twice as high). Most importantly, the duration of and the distance covered by the pole action are greater than in the kick. The average time of the kick phase in diagonal striding is between 0.12 and 0.20 seconds (this is 25 percent of the entire stride). The length of the push on the poles is between 0.31 and 0.63 seconds (approximately 66–70 percent). This means that the time span during which the arms' strength is used is on the average almost three times as long as that for the leg. *On the whole, the drive created by the arms in diagonal striding is approximately one-third the total drive created.* This means that about one-third of the forward movement is from the arms.

The angle formed by planting the pole (the pole angle) is quite large. The arm is in front of the body; thus, the "work conditions" are not good. Despite this, the downward push on the pole relieves the pressure exerted by the body's weight onto the ski by about one-sixth, lowering the friction between the ground and the ski. This stops any further drag on the ski at the end of the glide phase.

In actuality, the speed of the glide is slightly increased because of the mounting pressure exerted by poling. Poling, therefore, in conjunction with the forward swing of the leg, insures a constant glide speed between kicks.

Most Important Factors in Diagonal Striding:
- Proper arm and leg coordination
- Good gravity shift (flexed joints, center of gravity forward as far as possible)
- Start of the kick as early as possible
- Powerful kick, directed forward and up; constant pressure on the ground
- Good follow-through in the kick without overextending
- Complete weight shift onto the glide leg (one-leg gliding)
- Dynamic forward swing of the unburdened swing leg with full extension
- Powerful assistance from poling
- Slight forward lean of the upper body

The Worst Mistakes in Diagonal Striding

- Ambling; improper coordination, most often caused by planting the poles too early.
- Kick too late and too weak; most often in conjunction with "escape" steps.
- Center of gravity too far to the rear.
- Kick directed horizontally backward, no downward pressure—the drive is lost because of premature lifting of the ski.
- Poor extension of the legs.
- Active lifting of the calves instead of a relaxed back swing.
- No swing phase; the swing leg must support the body too soon.
- Exaggeration of the forward swing of the arms in planting the poles.
- Insufficient pressure exerted on the poles (no back extension of the arm/pole).
- Excessive arm movement (exaggerated forward swing, lateral deviations, high pole positioning from continuously gripping the poles firmly).
- Hyperextension of the arms or too much bend at the elbow.
- Major cause for many of the preceding mistakes—improper balance.

Diagonal Striding—Uphill

Providing that the uphill grade is not too steep, the diagonal stride is the most efficient and, therefore, the most frequently used technique. However, certain technical variations are necessary, depending upon the terrain.

It is obvious that inclines offer more resistance than level land. Wind resistance (not very strong in cross-country), friction, and force of gravity (F) all work against the skier. The effect of gravity is dependent upon the body weight (W) and the incline grade (α).

Explained in greater detail for those interested, this means $F = W \times \sin \alpha$. If, for example, you were to measure the resistance encountered on a flat run against a headwind of approximately 1 kilogram, the resistance would be around 3 kilograms, excluding the drag caused by friction. If the skier were climbing a 5° grade, the resistance would be 6 kilograms (with a bodyweight of 70 kg). At 10° the resistance increases to 12 kilograms. The resistance due to friction is less on an incline than on a level run, because there is less perpendicular pressure on the ski (formula: $N = W \times \cos \alpha$; see diag. 3). The decrease

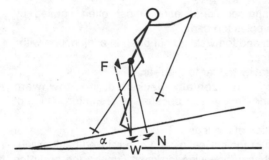

Diag. 3. Increased resistance in uphill diagonal striding.

in friction is very small (a few grams on a 5° incline). Its effect on the glide is minimal, although it does have a negative influence on the purchase potential.

To counterbalance the incline resistance, a more powerful and longer kick must be instituted. Although more power is added to the kick, the glide will not be increased because of the incline resistance. This shortening of the glide phase, sometimes a total absence of it on steeper grades, is to be expected.

These changes in the net effects of the strength expended result in lower values for the measurable time and distance per step of diagonal striding. The length of a cycle (excluding the glide phase) and the speed attained (slower, less efficient kick) decrease in value by about one-half. To ensure that the speed does not decrease too much, the time span per cycle is shortened and the step frequency is increased. This means more steps per unit of time.

There are also changes in the inner structure of diagonal striding that accompany those measurable external changes. Photo series 14 through 16 illustrate these inner characteristics.

PRE-KICK PHASE

The positioning of the body at the time of the gravity shift and the start of the kick is basically the same on level ground as on slight inclines (14/2, 15/2, and 16/2). The knee and ankle should be flexed slightly more to facilitate the follow-through of the kick leg. The lean of the upper body, however, is not increased. To do so would shift the body's center of gravity too far forward, decreasing the purchase of the ski.

KICK

The distance covered by the kick leg is approximately equal to that covered on level ground. As on level ground, the kick angle cannot be too small, without inviting the possibility that the ski will slip backward. Although the actual kick requires more strength, it lasts longer than a kick on level ground. Indeed, the steeper the incline, the longer the kick. Compare 15/5 and 15/6 to 16/5 and 16/6. In the sixth frame of both, the kick has just ended, although in 16/5 Georg Zipfel's swing leg is already closer to the glide leg than Peter Zipfel's in the same frame. Despite all this, Georg needs the same amount of time on a steeper incline to complete a shorter motion as Peter.

As the incline becomes steeper, the kick changes, becoming more of a leap up the hill, enabling the skier to maintain his forward motion. The kick becomes so powerful that the foot is lifted off the ground with the final push of the toes. The other leg (ski) is no longer pushed forward unburdened but is rather lifted slightly and swung forward. When properly executed, this creates a low ground-gaining leap forward with both feet momentarily airborne. Photo series 16 illustrates the transition between the glide and the leap steps. This technique should be continued as long as possible and as long as a minimum glide is achieved.

SWING PHASE

On level ground, the glide phase of one leg occurs simultaneously with the swing phase of the other. Because the glide phase is shortened in climbing, the swing phase must also be decreased. This is achieved by stopping full rear extension. In 14/5 and 15/5 the forward swing has just begun, although it is

14: Diagonal striding on level ground (Peter Zipfel).

15: Diagonal striding on a flat incline (Peter Zipfel).

16: Diagonal striding on a steep incline (Georg Zipfel).

17: Diagonal striding on a steep incline (Thomas Magnusson).

clear that Peter could have extended his leg more fully to the rear.

This means that the relaxed phase of the forward swing is dropped. Instead of an actively free forward swing after the kick or leap, the leg is pulled through. The knee is more bent than for level ground (compare 15/3 and 16/3 with 15/5, and 16/5 with 14/3). Although pulling the leg requires more time than the normal swing, the entire swing phase is faster because it is not necessary to fully extend the leg backward. Compare 15/4 and 15/5 with 16/4 and 16/5. In frame 4, Peter's kick leg is further back than Georg's, and, in frame 5, Georg's swing leg is further forward.

GLIDE PHASE

Parallel to the kick of one leg, the other leg is brought forward with uplifted heel and bent knee. This is to delay the weight shift for as long as possible (see 15/2, 15/4, 16/2, and 16/4). On steeper inclines the glide of the front leg is decreased after the gravity shift. However, to ensure that the kick is fully utilized and that each step covers as much ground as possible, the positioning of the calf as described on pages 77 and 78 becomes especially important. It is, therefore, more emphasized on inclines than on level ground (compare 14/1 to 14/3 with 16/1 to 16/3). If the incline requires the leap step, a weight shift onto the forward leg should occur after each leap. This shift should be completed quickly with the emphasis on the heel of the lead leg. Leaping augments the pressure exerted onto the ski, increasing the purchase.

18, 19: Diagonal striding on an incline (Magne Myrmo and Hans Speicher).

ARM/POLE ACTION

The most obvious differences between diagonal striding on level ground and on inclines are apparent in the arm/pole action. Just as the glide phase and the corresponding rear and front extensions of the legs are decreased on an incline, so are the movements of the arms. This consists primarily of shortening the front and back extensions intended to facilitate arm/leg coordination. An increase in the push phase is then substituted.

On flat ground the pole push is completed before the kick is over. On an incline the kick lasts longer, narrowing the interval between the kick and the pole push. Compare the sixth frame in photo series 14–16. On level land the pole has been clearly lifted by the end of the kick. On an incline the pole stays on the ground to provide support. The steeper the incline, the longer the pole remains planted, eventually ending simultaneously with the kick. The body is not pushed as far forward with the pole (compare photos 14, 15, and 16, frame 4). In the leap step the pole sometimes remains planted even briefly after the leap.

The pole is also planted earlier, before the end of the kick and the weight shift to the lead leg that follows. Once again: the steeper the incline, the earlier the planting. When leaping, the skier lands on the front leg and pole as he leaps from the other. He is then supported by the pole until the kick leg is brought forward and pressure is applied to the arm and leg. Because this causes the pole to be used longer in back of the body, there is a slight overlap between the beginning of one pole action and the end of the other. In comparing photos 15 and 16, frames 1 and 6, we see in 16/1 that as Georg begins his leg forward swing he has just completed his rear pole action. Peter, on the other hand,

20, 21: Diagonal striding on an incline (Sergei Savaliev).

is already swinging his pole forward. In 16/6 Georg is still
pushing on his right pole as he plants his left pole. Peter's rear
pole is in the same position as Georg's, but he is still swinging
his lead (right) pole forward. In comparing photos 18 and 19, it is
obvious that the elbow is bent more as the pole is planted,
because the body cannot glide past it as quickly on an incline
(see 15/1 and 16/1). Photo series 17 provides us with an
interesting comparison to photo 16. On the same incline, world
champion Thomas Magnusson, on this day out of form, appears
very tired compared to Georg Zipfel and his long, dynamic
strides (specifically compare 16/6 with 17/6). Sergei Savaliev,
the winner of this race, attacked this incline using long gliding
strides with a pronounced glide phase (photos 20 and 21).

22: Pendulum step—
"three-beat" (Juhani Repo).

Pendulum Steps

Why not pendulum step or pendulum gait or four-step or four-beat step or three-beat step? This should illustrate that among the experts the terminology can become very confusing. Sometimes the same term has different meanings because the individual words are illogical or misleading.

However, regardless of the terminology, everyone agrees that in diagonal striding it is sometimes necessary to omit one or more plantings of the poles. The time between plantings is taken up by swinging the poles slowly back and forth. This action is (to the Germans, at least) reminiscent of a clock's pendulum and is, therefore, called pendulum step (*pendelschritt*). This motion can be either regulated or unregulated. The simplest method is to allow one swing of the pendulum per kick if the pole is not to be used: hence, one *pendulum step*. There are several other possible variations; a number of kicks unsupported by poling is referred to in the plural as pendulum steps (*pendelschritte*).

The most common form is the pendulum step, used primarily in racing. It is used either within normal diagonal striding or as an interim in the transition from diagonal striding to double poling, or vice versa.

Photos 22/1 and 22/2 show a skier using diagonal striding technique. In 22/1 he has planted his right pole and has begun the swing phase; his left arm is swinging forward. In 22/2 he has completed his gravity shift in preparation for his left kick. In 22/3 he is entering the decisive phase. The left leg has just started to swing forward; the left pole should be planted. As the picture clearly illustrates, the pole tip is above the snow and somewhat to the rear. The forward swing was checked; the arm is slowly being moved forward. The hand is raised to ensure that the tips clear the ground. In photo 22/4, the right leg has begun its kick and the left pole has been checked, as it comes to the body. It will slowly be brought forward to a perpendicular position. In photo 22/5, the left hand has relaxed its grip on the pole to allow the tip to swing further forward. As the right pole is planted and the right leg begins the forward swing, the left pole tip also reaches its forward turning point. In photo 22/6, the gravity shifts for the left kick; the left pole has swung slowly backward and, reaching a perpendicular position, is lowered into action (here a bit early!). However, contrary to normal technique, the arm does not exert strong pressure at this point. In photo 22/7, the left leg and right pole are both beginning their forward swing; the skier begins to actively exert pressure on his left pole, returning to normal diagonal striding.

The left-pole action is omitted mid-stride, as the right leg kicks. The pendulum step, however, begins during the swing phase of the left leg and continues through to the start of the next (left) kick. It is, therefore, completed within three strides, the first and last of which were accompanied by poling action. This is the root of the most common name for the pendulum stride: *three-beat*.

Although rarely heard anymore, diagonal striding is some-times referred to as "two-beat." This means that every stride is accompanied by a poling action. Two (alternating) pole actions are exercised for every two strides in two beats. In three-beat, there are two pole actions for every three strides. In other words, there are two alternating pole actions in three beats. (Curiously, some people speak of "four-beat step" with three pole actions.) Finally, *"four-beat"* means two alternating pole actions for every pendulum swing of the arm (also known as "pendulum gait"—*pendelgang*). Diagram 4 clarifies this description.

(1)

two-beat (diagonal striding)

(2)

three-beat (one pendulum step—*pendelschritt*)
with alternating swing of the left and right poles

(3)

three-beat, with swinging on one side only

(4)

four-beat (two successive pendulum steps—*pendelschritte*)

Diag. 4. Pole actions in different strides.

Unfortunately, the borrowing of the word *beat* from music or engineering is not the best choice. In these two fields one speaks of notes or strokes, alternating regularly in timed succession, combined to form larger groups of equal length. Therefore only in those cases when a specific pendulum step is continued regularly over a longer course can we speak correctly of "three-beat" (or "four-beat").

Diag. 4a. Steady series of three-beat strides.

Diagram 4a shows a series of three-beat or even four-beat steps. These beats, perfectly ordered one after the other in a series, would rarely be used, even if a few normal diagonal strides were interspersed between the beats. (When the pictures of Juhani Repo in photo 22 were made, the Finn skied over 100 meters, interspersing three individual pendulum strides evenly over the distance, all with the right arm).

Generally speaking, the term *pendulum step* is used for single occurrences (see above). The terms *pendulum steps* ("three-beat") and *double pendulum step(s)* ("four-beat") are used to describe irregular occurrences.

Pendulum steps are used to allow the arms and back a respite on long level stretches or flat inclines. They are also used to avoid small obstacles on the track (tree stumps, etc.) or on poor poling surfaces (where poles penetrate too deeply). In traversing steep inclines, the uphill pole is not used.

Because of the widespread use of machines to prepare tracks, the need to use pendulum strides because of track conditions or to avoid obstacles is seldom necessary. In racing, because of the increased importance of poling, the pendulum stride is rarely if ever used. Even a few pendulum strides can result in a considerable loss of speed. The average speed attained during a three-beat series is about 6 percent less than the speed attained by diagonal striding, 9 percent less during four-beat!

As a result of this, the use of pendulum steps in racing (except for brief interims between technique changes) is almost nil. Pendulum steps are not used by light tourers because the steps would create coordination difficulties, even for good skiers. But the ability to properly execute pendulum steps is still the mark of a technically good skier.

Conclusion: Good skiers, and those who wish to become good skiers, rarely if ever use the pendulum step, and then only the three-beat variation unless course conditions demand. Racers should never use the pendulum step unless absolutely necessary.

If Using Pendulum Steps:

- Arm and leg coordination must remain fluid. Poor coordination generally results in balance difficulties.
- Keep legs moving in diagonal strides; above all, maintain equal drive.
- To facilitate the gravity shift that occurs immediately before the pendulum pole is put back into action, lean forward a bit more than usual.
- The arms and hands cannot be held too rigidly.
- The elbow must be bent a little more than usual and cannot have any lateral deviation.
- The pole must also remain parallel to the ski. Do not hold the pole firmly nor swing it wide.
- Do not hold the hand too high when swinging the pole forward nor turn the hand inward (for fear of jamming the pole into your stomach in case the tip catches!).
- Relax the grip on the pole.
- Do not plant the poles too far forward after ending the pendulum steps.

Double-Poling

The double-poling technique has always been the second most important method of propelling the cross-country skier forward after diagonal striding. Its application has steadily increased during the last few years. The desire to attain the fastest speed possible was greatly assisted by the introduction of new, faster materials for the construction of skis. A change to double poling on certain sections of a course that were previously covered by diagonal striding was also introduced for the sake of speed. Previously double poling was used mainly on fast downgrades and occasionally as a rest from diagonal striding. It is now used on level ground on tracks with good glide conditions. In addition, double poling provides valuable acceleration for the bow step *(bogenlauf)* and skating step. The use of double poling to provide rest intervals has greatly diminished because it creates excessive strain on the arms. In double poling, the arms, in conjunction with the upper body (shoulder, chest, and stomach musculature), are the sole means of forward drive. The legs are reduced to an inactive (support) status.

Double poling is the fastest means of moving forward on skis—downhill running excluded, naturally. By means of double

poling one can reach speeds on level ground of between 5 and 7.5 meters per second. One full push takes as long as two diagonal strides to complete, approximately 0.8 to 1.5 seconds, or 40 to 75 pushes per minute. Each shove covers between 4 and 7 meters more than one diagonal stride. It is interesting to note that the active push accounts for only 40 percent of the total time per push. The remaining 60 percent is consumed by the passive glide phase. The skier, despite the concentrated expenditure of energy required by the push phase, is not under constant strain as he is in diagonal striding.

The effectiveness of the double-poling technique is achieved through proper use of the poles (see diagonal striding, pp. 66 and 80). The pole is firmly planted in the snow, creating the

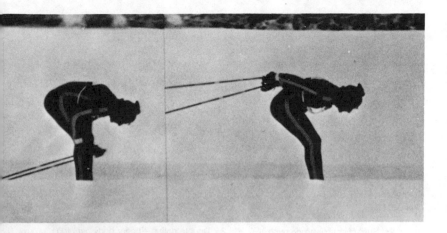

23: No-step double poling
(Walter Ziller).

most acute angle possible to cover the most ground per poling action. Both poles are planted and pushed simultaneously by the arms and the upper body.

Photo 23/1: The skier is extending his arms in preparation for the start of the double-poling action. The almost fully extended arms swing the poles simultaneously forward. How far forward he swings them depends on his tempo.

Photo 23/2: The upper body is bent forward, keeping the arms rigidly forward. This brings the poles into action. Again, how far forward the arms are brought is dependent upon the tempo. However, they are never brought so far forward that the planting angle (the angle between the ground and the front of the pole) is equal to or greater than 90°. The entire weight of the

24: Start of double-poling push (H. Speicher).

25: Double poling—upper body bent too far forward (Walter Ziller).

body is immediately applied to the poles, and the arms push powerfully backward. In so doing, *the elbows should be severely bent.* The hands remain relatively high and close to the body. Bending the arms transfers the weight of the body most efficiently to the arms and poles (short lever) and creates a 90° angle between the upper and lower arm. This right angle brings the triceps, the strongest muscles in the upper arm, into a position conducive to their full implementation. *The forearms should not be pushed downward (straightened) until the upper body is parallel to the ground.* The contraction of the triceps over a longer path provides better acceleration than if the elbows were held straight at the beginning, causing the hands to drop (compare with photo 24).

Photo 23/3: The follow-through of the forearms is intended to create the most acute pole angle possible (about 25°!), which in turn increases the potential horizontal drive. The hands should, therefore, be held as low as possible, below the knees, during the follow-through (clearly shown in 23/3). The push with the arms does not end until they are completely extended (see photo 25—although here, as in 23/3, the upper body is bent too far downward). At the end of the arm extension the hands open slightly as in diagonal striding to allow the poles to swing freely backward.

Photo 23/4: At the conclusion of the backward swing, the upper body, arms, and poles should form a relatively straight line. Starting with 23/1, we can observe that *the knees* (by appropriate muscle tension) *are held slightly bent throughout.*

26: Double poling—proper positioning of the upper body and head (Gerd-Dietmar Klause).

27: Double poling—improper positioning of the knees (Luigi Bonza).

The bend in the knees creates a rigid system that provides the optimum transfer of energy from the arms to the skis. *The feet should be as far forward of the hips as possible.* This allows the ski to glide faster.

The position of the body's center of gravity, far to the rear of the supporting structure, gives the impression that the skier must fall backward. The forward drive achieved by the push, together with the support provided by the feet on the skis, stops the skier from falling.

Photos 23/3 and 23/4 show improper head positioning. The skier should not look down at his feet, but rather should look in front of him as illustrated in photo 26.

Photos 23/5 to 23/7: The skier straightens his upper body in a *slow fluid movement,* bringing his poles forward in the same motion. A jerky, "hard" straightening of the upper body would decrease the pressure exerted on the ski considerably, increasing the friction and, therefore, the drag.

In 23/7 the skier has completed one cycle of double poling and has returned to his original position as in 23/1. It is common to see skiers with especially powerful double-poling technique throw their upper bodies forward at the end of a cycle (diag. 5) in conjunction with the start of the next cycle (planting of the poles).

Important: Breathing technique must be properly regulated. Inhale with the strengthening of the body; exhale as the upper body leans forward and the arms push on the poles.

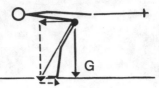

Diag. 5. Skier with very powerful double-poling technique.

Common Problems in Double Poling:

- Arched back at the start of the push
- Erect upper body during the push, "isolation"
- Upper body bent over too far during the push (see photo 25)
- Legs too relaxed: Flexibility or "give" in the legs in con-

28: One-step double poling (Thomas Wassberg).

junction with too great a bend in the knees that causes the body to drop, decreasing the efficiency of the push (see photo 27)

- Arms not fully extended to the run; hands held above the knees during the push (too large a pole angle)
- Straightening the body after the push either too late or too soon, and too jerkily

One-Step Double Poling

If the glide conditions on a slight incline or, more importantly, on level ground are such that the pure, or no-step, double-poling technique is either somewhat ineffective or too exhausting, you can add a step. This one-step double-poling technique is

excellent for flat or slightly rolling terrain and, therefore, is used more often than no-step double poling. It is frequently used on long race courses over flat terrain (uncommon in international competitions) covered with fast snow. Indeed, in these cases, it is common to ski over half the course using one-step double poling.

One-step double poling consists of a combination of no-step double poling and diagonal striding. The movement of the arms is almost identical to no-step double poling. This movement is then assisted by a kick borrowed almost directly from diagonal striding technique. These two movements are blended into a unified motion. In order to equalize the strain on the legs, it is good practice to alternate legs when kicking.

Under normal track and snow conditions, one specific style out of all of the various possibilities is generally used by all skiers. This is illustrated in photo 28.

Photos 28/1 to 28/3: The end of the push—the extension of the pole to the rear, the straightening of the upper body, and the forward swing of the poles associated with it—is the same as in no-step double poling (compare with photos 23/3 to 23/5). The only difference is in the positioning of the legs. The right leg, which has just completed its kick, remains behind the left leg. The bend in the knee (28/3) is noticeably less than in diagonal striding, where the forward-swing leg is brought parallel to the glide leg at the start of the gravity shift. The upper body does not become fully erect, as in no-step double poling (see 23/6), but is also not as far forward as in the gravity shift of diagonal striding.

29, 30: Start of the step in one-step double poling (Albert Giger).

31: Rear extension of the leg in double poling (Albert Giger).

Photo 28/4: The forward swing of the arms is carried higher; as the arms swing past the body, the left leg has started its kick. The forward swing of the arm and the kick become synchronized from this point on. To begin the kick, the ankle, knee, and hips are suddenly flexed (see photos 29 and 30). As a result of the relatively erect bearing of the upper body and the forward positioning of the left kick leg, pressure is exerted quickly onto the kick leg. The skier stamps forcefully onto the ground with the kick leg, thrusting his body up and forward (compare with the kick of diagonal striding, page 63). This effective kick (the purchase achieved appears to be better than that of diagonal striding—a ski that is too slippery for diagonal striding can be kicked effectively by one-step double poling on the same track)

32-35: Slight differences in body positioning in double poling (top: Magnusson; bottom: Myrmo and Giger).

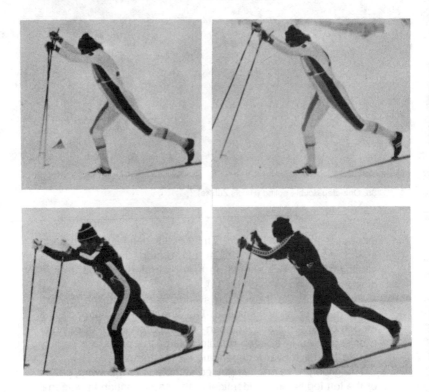

36: One-step double poling (Haldis Zühlke).

increases the overall speed. This occurs because the drop in speed during the glide phase of no-step double poling is eliminated. The kick should be fully extended backward as in diagonal striding (see photo 31).

Photo 28/5: As the left leg swings to the rear, the forward swing of the poles is continued. The simultaneous but opposing motion of the arms and legs can be compared to the opening of a scissors. As in no-step double poling, the poles are usually swung further forward, depending on the tempo.

The glide phase on the right leg at the end of the swing phase of the left leg is almost identical to the same motion in diagonal

striding (photos 32 and 33). Other skiers throw their upper bodies further forward (more vertical positioning of the thighs); compare photos 34, 35, and 36/6.

The poles are planted as the trail leg comes into contact with the ground on its forward swing. Naturally, the pole angle must be less than 90° (see 36/1). The coordination of the pole planting and the swinging of the legs is the same as that in diagonal striding (left or right). Thus, as the arms and legs reach their respective turning points in their swing phases (simultaneously), they begin their return movements (again simultaneously!).

Photo 28/6: The upper body and arm movements are again identical to no-step double poling. The movement of the forward-swing leg is also the same as in diagonal striding. The left swing leg has ended its forward swing (once again just behind the right leg), shortly before the arms sweep past the legs (see 36/2). Photoes 28/7 and 28/8 illustrate the push just after the positioning shown in 28/1 and 28/2. The cycle is complete.

The two photograph series and the accompanying explanation represent one-step double-poling technique at a normal frequency over a longer stretch. Certain changes must be made for a very high frequency (for instance, at the start or finish of a race). The rapid succession of movements does not allow for a deep forward bend of the upper body nor does it allow for an erect bearing at the end of a cycle. In addition, the follow-through of the kick is not as complete.

As mentioned previously, there are variations to this standardized style. The kick is often carried out in form only. Sometimes, usually because of poor snow or ski conditions, the time between the end of the kick and the start of the poling action is decreased. This means that the two actions can occur simultaneously or sometimes overlap. This is illustrated in diagram 6.

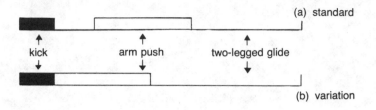

Diag. 6. Standard double-poling technique and variation.

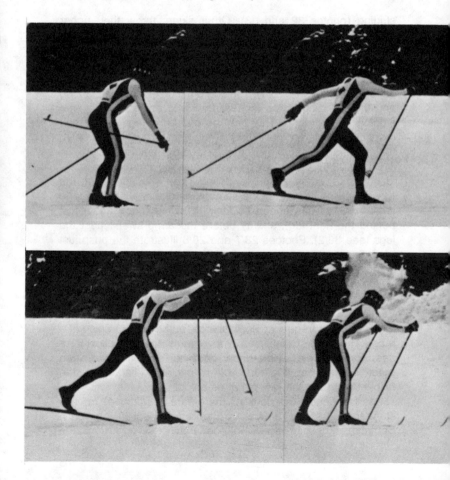

The diagram clearly illustrates that in the second case (the variation) the passive glide time is increased and the drop in speed must occur earlier. The standard form has the further advantage that the foot pressure corresponds in time to the end of the straightening of the upper body and the forward swing of the arms. It is only through this simultaneous coordination that the kick of the step leg achieves its full drive (see text to photo 28/4). The power of the kick in the variation form is approximately 15 percent less than in the standard form! This, in conjunction with the longer glide time, considerably reduces the potential top speed. On level ground a speed of up to 8.5 meters per second (30 kilometers per hour/18 MPH!) is possible, using the standard form. As we mentioned earlier, one-step double poling is excellent for courses with moguls, hills, and dips.

37: Transition from diagonal striding to double poling (Juhani Repo).

The kick should be timed to occur at the bottom of a dip. The ski will bow under the pressure of the kick, and the natural tension of the ski will then cause it to spring back again. If the skier kicks at precisely the right moment, he will be literally catapulted out of the dip and can then continue his poling. Using this technique, skiers with exceptionally strong arms can even fight their way up flat inclines.

Double poling with two or more steps is rarely used today. However if it is, the arm movements must be slowed accordingly to accommodate the time needed for the additional steps. The poles are planted, following the forward swing of the last step.

Transitions

Most cross-country courses, whether open terrain or difficult race tracks, are a combination of level, rising, and falling sections, to which the skier must constantly adapt. If an incline follows a slight downhill, the skier must change from double poling to diagonal striding. If the situation is reversed, the skier must shift from diagonal striding to double poling.

If the skier cannot make this transition smoothly, if he must interrupt his coordination, then his stride frequently will decrease for a moment. This means that his speed will decline and because of additional muscular activity he will also waste his strength and energy. In covering a 15-kilometer course, a good skier will change back and forth between these two techniques an average of 200 times, and on a 50-kilometer course, about 600 times. It is easy to see that even if the time lost were minimal it would be substantial over a long course.

Ideally, all transitions between diagonal striding and double poling (or the reverse) are accompanied by elements borrowed from pendulum steps. This ensures that the rhythm will not be disrupted. A clear break in the transition, a new beginning, so to speak, always disrupts the forward movement.

From Diagonal Striding to Double Poling

Photos 37/1 and 37/2: This is normal diagonal striding. In 37/2, the skier has reached the turning point in the rear extension of his right leg and left pole. The right pole should be planted as the right leg and left pole begin their forward swings. But, just as in the pendulum step, the right pole is also swung forward (see pages 79 and 90) for proper arm and pole movement).

Photo 37/3: In contrast of pendulum steps, most skiers swing the pole forward faster (as Repo does here). This means that they spread the full swing over more than one stride. In this frame the transition step between diagonal striding and double poling begins. This step differs from the step of normal one-step double poling only insofar as in this case one arm is already forward and only the other arm remains to be swung forward. The left arm and the right leg are in the middle of their forward swings, and the right arm has already ended its swing.

Photo 37/4: The right leg has ended its forward swing; the left arm has passed the body and continues in its forward swing while the left leg is just beginning its kick phase. (The continued forward movement of the right pole is actually an unnecessary reflex action.)

Photo 37/5: After kicking and following through, the left leg has reached its turning point. At the same time, the left arm has ended its forward swing and is not parallel to the right arm. The position achieved is identical to that of one-step double poling (compare with photo 28/5 and the text on page 102). This completes the transition, and the skier now continues normal double-poling technique (37/6 and 37/7).

From 37/3 on, the transition is, for all practical purposes, one-step double poling with an accelerated arm movement. Actually, up to 37/5 this could also be compared to a pendulum step. The only difference is that after 37/5 both poles—not just the left!—are planted.

If during the transition the skier is approaching the top of a rise that then drops off to a descent, he should try to time his movements so that the last stride before planting both poles ends at the crest of the rise.

38: Transition from no-step double poling to diagonal striding (Odvar Braa).

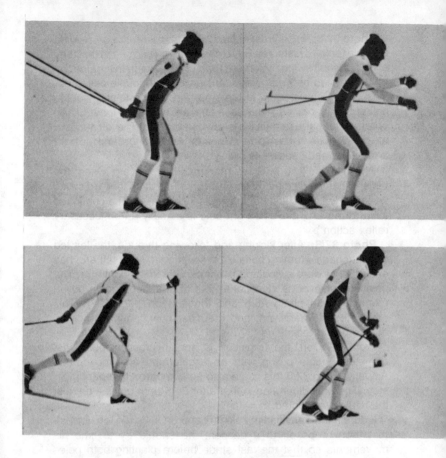

From Double Poling to Diagonal Striding

It is rare for a skier to go directly from double poling to diagonal striding.

Photos 38/1 and 38/2: After completing the push, the skier has straightened up and swung his arms and poles forward as if he were going to continue double poling. The pole tips are directed slightly forward.

Photo 38/3: The left arm and pole are held briefly in the position of 38/2. As the left leg kicks, the right pole swings forward as in pendulum steps.

Photo 38/4: After completing the kick and follow-through, the left leg swings forward again. The left pole is planted as the forward swing begins. The right pole is still swinging forward. From this point on, all of the movements are identical with the

39: Transition from one-step double poling to diagonal striding (Thomas Magnusson).

last stage of pendulum steps (see page 90 and photo 22/5). and the skier can continue in normal diagonal striding technique.

This transition usually begins with one-step double poling.

Photo 39/1: The skier has just straightened up after completing the last push.

Photo 39/2: The transition begins exactly as in one-step double poling. The skier kicks with his left leg as he swings both his arms forward.

Photo 39/3: After the skier completes the kick and follow-through of the left leg and the forward swing of the left pole (compare photo 32), the left leg begins to swing forward again. If the transition were from no-step double poling, both poles would be planted at this point. In this case, however, only the left pole is planted. The right pole swings forward. From this point, as just explained for photo 38/4, the movements are the same as for the

40: Transition from one-step double poling to diagonal striding (Frantisek Simon).

last stage of pendulum steps. From 39/5 on (planting of the right pole), the skier can use double-poling technique (see photo 40).

If, after pushing off on his poles, the skier encounters a curve or a dip leading into an incline, he must be erect before he enters the curve or dip. He should kick powerfully through the dip and begin the forward swing of his arms. (If he were to enter the dip with his body still bent forward or if he were to push on his poles while in the dip, he could crash his skis into the far side of the dip.) Instead the skier pulls himself through the dip by swinging both his arms forward and by kicking.

Herringbone

Diagonal striding is the most commonly used technique for climbing inclines. However, if the grade is too steep to climb up with the skis straight or if the conditions are such that the ski has little purchase, it is best to change to herringbone technique.

In this technique the fronts of the skis are turned out (the ends remain close together). The knees are not only bent forward but also turned inward so that the inside edge of the ski cuts into the snow. With one ski held firmly to the ground, the other ski is lifted just enough to clear the snow and then set down again in a position parallel to its previous position. This motion is continued, alternating skis, with the appropriate shifting of weight from one ski to the other. This leaves a herringbone pattern in the snow.

The poles are also used alternately in the manner of diagonal-striding poling. Thus, if the skier's weight is on his left leg to enable him to move his right leg forward, he then plants his right pole behind the ski. The left arm swings forward with the forward movement of the right ski. This coordination facilitates a smooth transition from diagonal striding to herringbone. The change from one technique to the other must be timed properly,

before the skis start to slide backward during diagonal striding. This assumes prior knowledge of which grades can be climbed with your skis pointing straight ahead.

You can either trudge slowly up a hill using the herringbone technique or spring up the hill with powerful drawn-out kicks. On racecourses with long steep hills, where you must use the herringbone technique, it is common for even world-class skiers to scale them relatively slowly to ensure that at the end of the hill they can continue with full tempo. Herringbone is more demanding than leaping in diagonal striding.

The steeper the hill, the wider the fronts of the skis are held apart, the shorter the step, and the more the skier supports himself on the poles planted as far back behind the body as possible. The upper body should not lean too far forward.

41: Herringbone (Peter Zipfel).

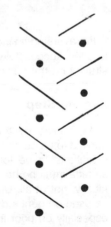

Diag. 7. Half-herringbone technique.

111

In traversing an incline, a *half-herringbone technique* (diag. 7) is often successfully used. In this case, the uphill ski is held straight on the track and the downhill ski is pointed outward.

Skating Step

As implied by the name, this is an ice-skating technique applied to cross-country skiing. It is not necessary, however, for conditions to be totally icy to use this technique. The snow surface must be hard, so that the ski sinks in only minimally or, ideally, not at all. Under these conditions, the skating step can be used on gentle downslopes, flats, or even slight uphills, and especially on poor tracks, to greatly increase the tempo.

The basics of this technique are similar to the herringbone. The fronts of the skis are almost pointing outward. As in the

42: Skating step
(Sigi Maier).

herringbone, the body's weight is shifted completely to the ski
that is kicking. The knee is also turned inward to allow the inside
edge of the ski to bite the snow. In the skating step, however, the
knee is sharply bent in preparation for the kick.

To kick, the leg is straightened powerfully, angled slightly
outward, pushing the body in the direction of the opposite ski,
which is lifted and angled outward. This motion should be
carried through by the entire body. The arms, which are held in
tight next to the legs at the start of the kick, should be swung
powerfully forward in the direction of the lead ski, pulling the
body with it. As soon as the ski is set down, the entire body
weight should shift to it. The kick ski can be left where it is.
However, to ensure a proper shift to the glide ski, it is better to
pull it up close to the kick ski (almost parallel). It is important that
the kick ski remain on the ground until it becomes the glide ski

and must be lifted forward. With the skier standing relatively upright, directly over the ski, the glide should be carried out until the loss in speed becomes too great. Then the body should be crouched again—that is, the ankle and knee should be bent, the arms pulled back tight to the body—and the kick started as the new glide ski is lifted forward and the other leg kicks.

The already considerable acceleration resulting from the technique can be further increased when used in conjunction with double poling. In this case, maximum efficiency is attained when a step is added to the poling action. The arms swing forward (as just described) with the kick and then, depending upon the speed, you remain upright on the skis briefly and then plant both poles and push. In contrast to double poling, with the skis parallel to one another, the knee of the glide leg should also be bent for the push and forward lean of the upper body. This not only achieves an increase in stability but also causes the body to end up in the crouched position necessary for the start of the next kick at the end of the push phase. The proper rhythm is shown in diagram 8: kick (body upright)—push ("crouching")—kick—push, and so on.

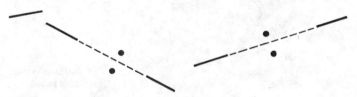

Diag. 8. Skating step.

This coordination helps establish your balance but means that you glide for long distances, sometimes up to 30 feet on one ski! If glide conditions are bad, creating balance difficulties, the push and the kick may be executed simultaneously (shortening the length and time of each step).

Despite the long glide, this technique is very tiring, demanding strength in both the kick and the glide phases. However, especially on a level, frozen surface (next to the track), with slick skis, the skier using this technique will leave those using diagonal striding or double poling slipping in their tracks. Experienced skiers with strong arms prove the effectiveness of this technique even on short flat inclines.

A rarely seen but very effective variation of this technique is a one-sided, one-legged skating step (see diag. 9), which we call

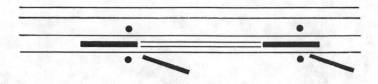

Diag. 9. Half-skating step.

the *half-skating step.* One ski is kept on the track (especially if the track is firm and deep), and ideally the left ski is angled outward and kicked, supported by simultaneously planting both poles.

Bow Step

If a change in direction is necessary on level or slightly falling terrain that is too sharp for a normal track to follow, you must switch to the bow-step *(bogentreten)* technique. As the name implies, (*bow*—one thinks of a curve), you "step" through the curve.

You still kick with one ski (the outside ski in relation to the curve), turning and lifting the other ski in the direction of the curve. Upon setting this glide ski down, the outside ski is immediately pushed parallel to it. The kick from this outside ski is identical to the kick of the skating step technique. This means that with body weight completely on the outside ski, knee bent inward, ankle and knee well bent, you lift and aim the inside ski inward (with the curve). Kick off the inside edge of the outside ski and then pull through with it toward the inside ski. The arms should be thrown forward with the kick, "pulling" the body with them.

The essential difference from the skating step is that the inside ski, pointed outward, does not "bite" with its inside edge but rather with its outside edge. Because the terms *inside* and *outside* could be misleading, diagram 10 should prove useful.

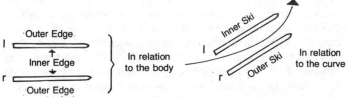

Diag. 10. Bow step, showing inside ski biting with outer edge.

The body's entire weight is immediately shifted to the inside ski. The outside ski can now be lifted and placed parallel to the inside ski. As soon as the outside ski comes into contact with the ground, the entire body weight is shifted back onto it.

On longer curves, the kick and extension of the kick leg leads to a noticeable increase in speed. The body will follow the inward extension of the kick leg and will be relatively upright on the inside ski. When the body weight is shifted back onto the outside ski, the body crouches again. A double-poling push at this point will give a burst of acceleration. The poles are most effective if planted simultaneously with the placing of the outside ski parallel to the inside ski as the body begins to crouch. The glide is basically on the outside ski, because the inside ski must be lifted and aimed once again.

43: Bow steps (Sigi Maier)

It is naturally not possible to execute this type of powerful kick step with its strong kick, pole push, and long glide on short, tight curves. For such curves, the body remains low with bent knees, the steps are shortened, and the weight shifts are quicker. Knowing exactly when to kick (diag. 11a) and exactly where to aim the inside ski comes with experience, especially if the track is hard, deep, and fast.

A properly executed bow step is marked by "true" tracking in a straight line on the weighted ski. This is not possible at high speeds unless not only the knee bends forward and in but also the upper body leans, creating added pressure on the biting ski edge. If this is not done, then the ski will slip and slide outward. This results in a lengthening of the curve radius, a loss in speed, and an increased likelihood of a fall.

Diag. 11. Bow running technique.

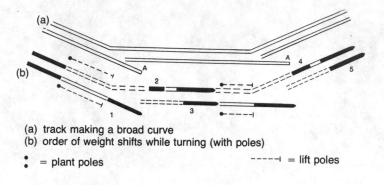

(a) track making a broad curve
(b) order of weight shifts while turning (with poles)

⋮ = plant poles   - - - - -⊣ = lift poles

Bow Running

The technique we have just described, bow steps, allows you to change direction even on slightly rising terrain, especially (as is often the case) when the slight incline is at the bottom of a downhill run and is introduced by a curve. As a rule, however, directional changes on inclines are accomplished by using the *bow running (bogenlaufen)* technique.

This entails the integration of normal diagonal striding into bow running. The only difference is that the skis are constantly shifting from the original direction of the kick. When the outside ski is extended backward, the leg is turned slightly inward,

Diag. 12. Using bow running to turn.

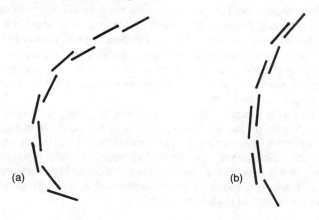

forcing the rear of the ski outward. As the ski is swung forward (or pushed forward unburdened), the front of the ski points somewhat inward. The inside ski is also directed slightly inward (into the curve) by turning the inside leg outward at the turning point of its rear extension (diag. 12a). If the curve is not too sharp, it is not necessary to turn the inside ski inward; it is sufficient to turn the outside ski and set the inside ski down parallel to it (diag. 12b). This technique is for both gliding steps and "springing" steps.

Because almost all race courses are now mechanically prepared, technical refinements such as bow running and especially bow step are rarely necessary, but valuable tools for a racer when needed.

Downhill Running

Whoever wishes to ski over varied terrain on cross-country skis must also be able to ski downhill. For most skiers, this offers a welcome rest; for others, a horror. Even good Alpine skiers are initially alarmed when they consider downhill skiing on such narrow skis and free-moving heels. Actually it is only a question of personal confidence and expectations and a knowledge of condition and lay of the track.

Skiing Along the Fall Line

To ski the fall line, skis should be held at hip-width. Ankles, knees, and hips are bent; this means knees are pushed forward

44: Downhill running—crouch position (Toni Reiter).

somewhat, something that is very important, and hips are relatively low. This should create the sensation that the entire foot is evenly pressed to the ski. The arms should be bent, with the elbows directed slightly outward to help maintain balance. Keep the pole tips behind the body.

Most of the effects of uneven ground are absorbed by the legs, which should be straightened slightly in dips and bent more over rises. Allow the legs to be "pushed" up.

Skiers who enjoy speed assume the tuck position. This has many forms, ranging from a slight bend of the knees to a full crouch, the "egg" position made popular by downhill racers. Generally the knees are pushed as far forward as possible, the thighs are held somewhat horizontally, and the upper body is bent down over the thighs. The elbows may be rested on the thighs. Poles should be held loosely between the arms and the body, pointing to the rear.

To slow the tempo, you may stand more erect, holding the arms away from the body to the sides. If the snow is deep, it is possible to ski alongside the track, allowing the deep snow to act as a brake. It is advisable to change from the track to the side before you have gained too much speed. Only the most stable skiers can jump a track at high speeds. And even then, there is a good chance the deep snow will slow you down so quickly you will fall forward. In any case, you should lift one ski at a time while leaning back slightly on the other in going from the track to the side of it.

45: Downhill running—snowplow (Toni Reiter).

Stopping and Turning

Skiers may always use the snowplow to stop. This is done by turning the already bent knees inward, turning the heels out, and standing on the inside edge of the skis; this forms the plow. Even the most experienced skiers are not ashamed to snowplow when they are on a steep or blind slope (see photo 49).

Turning on downhill runs is usually accomplished using bow steps. It is also possible to go through curves using the snowplow, shifting the weight primarily onto the outside ski, bending the outside knee and turning it inward. On prepared tracks it is not usually necessary to traverse down a hill. However traversing is possible and on relatively firm ground with good purchase this can be done quite well. It is not recommended on icy slopes, on broken frozen snow, or slush. Under favorable conditions it can be truly enjoyable to ski in an Alpine manner on cross-country skis.

Many cross-country books recommend that skiers lean backward when downhill running in order to avoid lateral movement of the heel. This is completely wrong. On the contrary, you should not ski in this "easy chair" position. The body's center of gravity should be squarely over the feet. This is the only correct positioning. It is only in this middle position that you may remain stable and traverse a hill. Because cross-country boots are not high and rigid, skiers may fully utilize the flexibility of the ankles and knees.

46: Traversing on cross-country skis — turning with a modified stem christie (Sigi Maier).

47: Traversing (Sigi Maier).

48: Traversing (Sigi Maier).

Developing Technique and Style

In comparison to other sports in which new, revolutionary developments in technique result in ever-increasing levels of achievement (for example, in the high jump: scissors, roll, straddle, and now flop techniques), cross-country skiing is relatively conservative. All of the previously described techniques have been well established since the introduction of racing at the turn of the century. Even within the various techniques themselves, little has changed. Some such changes are the pushing forward of the lower leg in diagonal striding or the straight, stiff position of the legs instead of a deep crouch in double poling. Such changes are essentially the results of improvements in condition factors.

It is clearly with these changes in mind that we speak of modern (or present-day) cross-country technique. Modern cross-country technique is noted for its athletic character.

Modern Cross-Country Technique:
- High frequency of steps
- Early, dynamic kick
- Accentuated forward and back swing
- Relatively erect posture
- Increase in arm/pole action
- Increasing significance of double poling

Whenever an athlete masters a specific technique within a sport but does not execute it "by the book," preferring to add his own personal variations, we speak of his particular style. Photo 8 does not illustrate specific elements of style, however, but, rather, technical mistakes. Similarly, photo 27 illustrates what was previously considered to be a question of style but, according to modern technique, is now viewed as technically incorrect.

Within cross-country skiing there has always been considerable room for variation in style. Stylistic differences, assuming technical accuracy, are for all practical purposes irrelevant in determining performance levels. The differences in performance are almost totally dependent upon conditioning. High stride frequency and an explosive kick and pole push in conjunction with long glides are the building blocks of high performance.

49, 50: A comparison in styles of diagonal striding: *top row:* Gerd-Dietmar Klause; *bottom row:* Thomas Wassberg.

Nevertheless, it should prove interesting to end this section on technique by illustrating some stylistic differences among world-class skiers. Our intent, however, is not merely to show aesthetic differences in style, but also variations from the standard technique according to the terrain. Photos 49 and 50 show the second- and third-place finishers of a race (Reit im Winkl, 1977) on a slight incline: second place—G. Klause (East Germany, Olympic Silver medalist, 1976, 50 km); third place—T. Wassberg (Sweden, World Cup champion, 1977).

Photos 49/1 and 50/1: Start of the kick.

Photos 49/2 and 50/2: Near the end of the kick (Klause just finished, Thomas Wassberg not quite).

Photos 49/3 and 50/3: Start of the forward swing of the kick leg. It is most interesting to compare the differences in their upper bodies. Wassberg is bent forward whereas Klause is relatively erect. It is also interesting to note the low arc drawn by Klause's somewhat extended arms.

51: A comparison of techniques: diagonal striding and double poling on the same terrain: *left:* Sven-Ake Lundbäck, *right:* Odvar Braa.

Photos 51/1 to 51/6: These show the use of the different techniques by two skiers on the same stretch of course. (These two skiers were racing neck and neck at the time.) In 51-6 Sven Lundbäck (Sweden) has just completed one cycle of diagonal striding, while Oddvar Bra (Norway) has not quite completed a double-poling push.

52: Diagonal striding—different tempos: *from left to right:* G. Zipfel and Oberholzer, P. Zipfel and J. Vogel.

Photo series 52: This shows two pairs of skiers. In the first picture, the first pair has synchronized the planting of their right poles, while the second pair is in the middle of kicking with their left legs. Following the series to 52/8 (two seconds later), we can see that the second pair is still synchronized and is now only half a step out of "sync" with Oberholzer, while G. Zipfel is half a step further is his cycle and is now, thus, in sync with the second pair.

Training

Central to the complex term *training* is the issue of performance. Everyone who cross-country skis regularly has attained a certain level of performance and probably has aspirations for an even higher level. Without a doubt, better performance also means more enjoyable skiing.

At the conclusion of the previous section, it was mentioned that good technique is not possible without good conditioning. Anyone wishing to cross-country ski seriously must concern himself or herself with the element of training.

A good training program embraces your entire person, and because each person is different—age, condition, time, location, and so on—training programs must be tailored to fit the individual. In contrast to the previously offered details on technique, here we can provide only the framework of a training program that would be useful for general conditioning, as well as that specifically for cross-country skiing.

The main goal of training is to raise your level of performance to its highest degree attainable, based on your ability and your preparedness. Ability involves your body conditioning and technical, tactical, and intellectual sharpness. Preparedness is psychological. The foundations for both ability and preparedness are developed by making steady demands, using specific training means and according to different training methods. This development must not be arbitrary or purposeless, but rather, well planned, according to specific principles.

The most important factor in a good training program is having an individually designed, long-lasting program that involves a systematic increase in demand, coordinated with the changing seasons. You should train throughout the year, with your goal being that of increasing your level of performance each skiing season. The specific training program you choose depends upon your age and sex, together with the length of time you may previously have trained and your general level of training.

In Table 1, the most important aspects of a systematic training schedule are given. This overview is naturally designed to meet the particular needs of the cross-country skier, and it clearly illustrates that the term *condition* is multifaceted.

TABLE 1

TRAINING—A SYSTEMATIC OVERVIEW

Training Fundamentals (methods)	Training Forms (exercises and training)
Conditioning	

General

state of health	medical checkup, hygiene, clothing, diet, rest
general physical development	gymnastics, track, swimming, games, hiking, mountain climbing, cycling, rowing, canoeing, etc.

Physical Factors

strength	circuit training, dumbbells, weight pulleys (increase repetitions, not weights)
speed	reflex exercises, springs (up to 50 m)
speed strength (spring power)	leaping strides (up to 50 m, increased speed, longer rest periods), jumping exercises for one and two legs (leap-frogging over obstacles, hopping, etc.)
endurance	
general and aerobic endurance	cross-country running, street running (roller skis)
speed endurance (anaerobic)	tempo runs: 400-1,000 m (repetition method, few repetitions with long rest periods)—over 1,000 m generally only 1 run; street running with springs; hill climbs (on foot, roller skies, or cross-country skis)
strength endurance (individual muscle groups)	leaping strides (30-60 seconds), hill runs (30-120 seconds), circuit training,

weight pulleys (short rest periods, low repetitions at high weights and high repetitions at low weights), mountain climbs and runs over 30 minutes, roller skis, mountain runs (diagonal), no-step double poling

Motor Skills

mobility — gymnastics (stretching, flexibility)

agility and balance — games (volleyball, basketball, soccer—with caution), obstacle-course running, one-legged exercises (hopping, rotations, gliding)

Psychological Conditioning — psychological preparedness: attitude, motivation, desire

---

Technique

Technique Training — technique practice on skis, imitative exercises (leaping strides, roller skis)

Tactics

Tactical Training and *Tactical and Theoretical Knowledge* — knowledge of the rules of competition, of the care and use of equipment, of waxing, of training methods, observing the track before the race, and others

---

Other Considerations

Training Demands

Physical load	Difficulty ⌈intensity ⌊extent	Training frequency

Training Methods

Endurance ⌈continuous ⌊varying ⌊*fartlich*	Interval Repetition Competition and control

136

Training Periods

Summer		preparatory	Stages	microcycle
Fall	Periods	competition		macrocycle
Winter		transition		
Spring				

Training Classes and Levels

Children	Male	Fundamental (basic)
Youth	Female	Developmental (intermediate)
Adult		High performance (advanced)

It is imperative for every type of training that you be in good health, supported by regular checkups. If sick, you should first consult with a doctor before training and then engage only in light training. A steady, continuous increase in performance levels due to a special training program is not guaranteed unless your entire body is strengthened through a thorough preliminary program (see Training Classes and Levels). The general exercises of such a program are occasionally used in specialized training programs.

Performance Factors—Conditioning

This specialized condition training builds the physical and psychological capabilities necessary for sports, among them cross-country skiing. The so-called physical factors are basically dependent upon muscular activity; good motor skills are the mark of a well-functioning nervous system, which controls the body's movements. The basic physical factors—strength, speed, speed strength, and endurance—combine to form complex external characteristics.

Strength, Speed, Speed Strength, and Endurance

Strength: The ability of the muscles to contract against an opposing force and to cause the opposing force to move (dynamic strength—for example, to lift a weight). It also is the ability of contracted muscles to resist an opposing force (static = stable power—for example, to hold a weight in an uplifted position). Cross-country skiing utilizes far more dynamic strength, although static strength is used in the glide phase and during downhill runs (upper thighs). *Maximum strength,* or *absolute strength* (the highest possible use of muscular strength against an opposing force), is of little significance in cross-country skiing. The strength factors of speed and endurance are much more important.

Speed: The ability to move as quickly as possible. There are two factors at work here: *reflex speed* (time lapse between a stimulus and a reaction) and *overall speed in movement*. As with strength, the highest possible or absolute speed attainable is not significant in cross-country skiing. In related forms, however, they are very important. These related forms are speed strength and speed endurance.

Speed strength: The ability of the muscles to move as quickly as possible against an opposing force. This determines the strength and explosiveness of the cross-country kick and, in conjunction with other performance factors, allows for long strides and a high stride frequency.

Endurance: The ability to carry out an athletic movement for the longest period possible without tiring. Fatigue results in quantitative and qualitative decreases in movement. These mean poorer coordination (technique and efficiency) and a loss in speed. Endurance is decisive for performance in cross-country in all of its various manifestations.

Endurance can be either aerobic or anaerobic. *Aerobic* (*aer* is Greek for *air*) means that during the physical activity of the muscles (or other parts of the body), oxygen is present in sufficient quantities for the consumption of energy. The balance between the supply and demand of oxygen is known as the steady-state condition. Naturally, as the intensity of the exercise increases, so does the oxygen demand. Longer distances must be covered in this steady state condition, but at not too fast a tempo to ensure that fatigue does not become overpowering. In such cases (eight minutes and longer), we speak of long-lived endurance. This primary type of endurance, the ability of the body to resist fatigue over longer distances through aerobic activity, is usually referred to as *general endurance* (also *basic endurance*). This type of endurance is of primary importance in cross-country skiing (shortest races: 5 km for women—fastest times around fifteen minutes).

Various Forms of Endurance

Over shorter distances, different types of endurance come into play. The endurance necessary to cover distances about eight to two minutes is referred to as *mid-lived endurance*. *Short-lived endurance* covers the times between about two minutes and forty-five seconds. The shorter the time, the higher the intensity that can be chosen. In these cases, the energy consumption is primarily anaerobic. *Anaerobic* means that it is not possible to provide the body with enough oxygen to satisfy the oxygen demand. The energy supply (basically glycogen—sugar) is broken down without oxygen (producing lactic acid). This "oxygen-debt" condition can be maintained, without causing total fatigue, until the muscles become "saturated" with lactic acid.

The ability of the body to resist fatigue over short periods of time at high or extreme levels of intensity (speed) is also known as *speed endurance* (stay power). (This term can also be used to denote mid- and short-lived endurance in many instances.) In cross-country skiing, speed endurance is very important because, although the average race is quite long, individual sections of a course (inclines) demand a high level of intensity over a short period of time where speed loss is not too great.

General endurance and speed endurance are basically abilities of the entire body (heart, circulatory system, lungs, and metabolism). Another type of endurance is *strength endurance*. This type of endurance is reflected in good general endurance, but more specifically in the ability of individual muscle groups, in this case the muscles used in cross-country skiing, those that are constantly working against opposing forces, to resist fatigue in providing strength for long periods of time. This type of endurance is also relatively important in skiing on inclines and during long stretches of double poling. The "special" (also known as "special competition") endurance of cross-country skiers (in contrast to the same for runners, swimmers, etc.) is based on all of the individual endurance types mentioned. It is imperative that all cross-country skiers, regardless of level, have good general endurance. The higher the level of performance desired, the more the skier must concentrate on strength and speed-endurance training.

Motor Skills

Together with these physical performance factors, motor skills form the basis of all performance. The motor skills are mobility, agility, and balance.

Mobility: The ability to utilize the full range of movement of the joints (also known as flexibility). This is naturally not as important in cross-country skiing as in other sports (for instance, gymnastics). However, insufficient mobility hampers the full realization of other body capabilities, such as endurance, strength, speed, and agility.

Agility: The result of good coordination and control of the trunk and limbs (total movement), seen from three prospectives: the ability to learn quickly an athletic move; the ability to master quickly a difficult movement; and, finally, the ability to execute these movements under all circumstances, including the ability to adapt quickly. In cross-country skiing, agility is particularly necessary in properly executing various technique forms on changing terrain.

Balance: The ability either at a standstill or in movement to maintain your balance (static and dynamic balance). In cross-country skiing, it is not possible to glide without dynamic balance (on both legs, but even more importantly on one leg). The close relationship of balance to the other motor skills is illustrated, for example, when a cross-country skier loses his balance on a downhill run. In order to regain his balance, he needs good reflexes, agility, and extra strength.

All of these physical performance factors and motor skills must be trained equally. If one factor is especially weak, the training program must be altered to bring it up to par with the other factors.

Training Demands

Before we go on to discuss the training methods used to develop these fundamental factors, we must provide a better understanding of the interconnection between these factors and the demands of training.

With the help of training, the body functions will be stimulated. This stimulation affects the appropriate systems (heart, musculature, psyche, etc.), causing them to adapt to the situation, whether it is of minimal intensity or approaching maximum value. Proper doses of intensity create demands on the body that cause fatigue (energy consumption). In the rest periods following a training workout the energy reserves are not only replenished to their previous levels but are filled to a higher level (overcompensation).

> **A Few Important Conclusions:**
> - Physical demands and rest periods must be properly coordinated.
> - If the periods between training workouts are too long, the body's capacity to adapt decreases.
> - Continuous invariable physical demand does not increase the capacity to adapt and, therefore, has no further training benefits. Physical demand must be constantly increased.
> - A smooth, even increase on physical demand is not as effective as an incremental one. The relatively high increase that occurs after a specific time period because of the extensive breakdown of tissues causes the body to overcompensate, increasing the level of performance attainable.

It is possible to control accurately the physical demands placed on the individual organs and their interrelationships. In the portion on health (pages 25–34) the effects of physical demands on the body characteristic to cross-country skiing and the desired manifestations of an increase in adaptive capacity were discussed in detail. In the following section the components of creating physical demands are discussed.

Intensity of Demand

Intensity of demand refers to the level of performance achieved within a specific time period—the higher the level in the same time span, the higher the intensity. In track and field, the intensity and speed of a race run on level ground are one and the same. In cross-country, however, the intensity is determined by the relative speed. For example, although the top speed attained on an incline is less than on flat ground, in order to ensure that the speed does not decrease too greatly, the intensity must be increased. It is essential to any training program that the skier constantly change the intensity of his workouts. The range of intensity a skier can work with is determined by the top speed a given skier can attain in relation to his pulse rate. The highest intensity (100 percent) is 180 pulse beats or more per minute. Lesser intensity (approximately 40 percent and below) is 120 pulse beats or less per minute. The latter has little effect, however, in endurance training. Between these two values there are gradations: moderate intensity (120–140 pulse beats/minute), medium intensity (140–160 pulse beats/minute), and submaximum intensity (160–180 pulse beats/minute). Table 2 clearly illustrates these values.

TABLE 2
INTENSITY LEVELS WITH CORRESPONDING PULSE BEATS

	moderate		medium	sub-maximum		maximum
Pulse beats/minute	130	140	⌐150⌐	160	170	⌐180⌐
Approximate intensity	50%	60%	70%	80%	90%	100%

It is also important for the cross-country skier to know:

- Improvements in the cardiovascular system do not occur below 130 pulse beats/minute.

- Based on this information, a training program that properly coordinates all of the body's systems should guarantee the skier maximum aerobic capacity. This means that the skier should be able to maintain a sufficient oxygen level over a long period of time to ensure that the lactic acid buildup will not be too great. This is best achieved by training at an intensity level between the medium and submaximum levels. This means 160 pulse beats per minute with a plus/minus variable of 10. Long distances should be generally (but not always!) run at this intensity.

- The skier's workout should also include periods of maximum intensity with high anaerobic demands (specifically on inclines), which increase the lactic acid buildup without fatiguing the skier to the point that he can't continue. This implies that a training program must include runs that demand submaximum and maximum intensity tasks.

- Additionally, the relationship between the intensity and continuity of training is significant. A continuous, relatively low intensity in training will result in a slow increase in the performance potential, which will level out. Higher intensity will result in faster improvement in the performance potential but will not hold steady. This why it is necessary first to establish a stable condition based on moderate and medium intensity training before training at the submaximum level.

The Extent of Physical Demand (Duration)

The extent of physical demand is the sum of the total work completed within one *training unit* (TU). Cross-country training usually consists of uninterrupted endurance training. In this case, the extent of the training is equivalent to the time spent training. However, if the training includes rest periods with repetitions, the extent of the physical demand is the time needed per repetition multiplied by the number of repetitions.

Close interrelationships exist between the extent and the intensity of the physical load. The relationship must ensure that the physical demand created by one TU is sufficient, not excessive. With respect to individual TUs, the extent (duration) of the TU must be high (long, if the intensity is low. Beginning with long-lasting, low-intensity workouts, it is possible to increase both the length and the intensity of the workout. The duration and intensity of a workout are dependent upon the level of conditioning. The higher the conditioning level, the longer and more intense the workout, increasing the performance potential.

In order to achieve the special goals of cross-country, training workouts must not drop below a minimum physical demand period. To improve the general aerobic endurance capacity, a beginning skier must work out at least ten to twelve minutes at a medium-intensity level. For individuals with previous training, workouts should be no less than thirty minutes at the same intensity level. Skiers who wish to compete regularly should train regularly for periods (not necessarily distances) 10 to 20 percent longer than normal races (15–30 km). This means one to two hours of training. Top racers usually train up to three hours per TU.

Anaerobic endurance training with submaximum and maximum intensity should be no less than ten minutes total duration per TU. This training can be (and often is) broken down into smaller time blocks of one to two minutes duration.

The Relationship between Physical Demand and Recovery

The body's ability to adapt to changing physical demands is increased during the recovery period. The broader the extent and the greater the intensity of the physical demand, the longer the recovery period needed to allow the energy reserves to replenish themselves to their former levels and beyond (overcompensation). For this reason, you should plan TUs with long endurance training at medium- and submaximum-intensity levels to be followed immediately by a hard anaerobic training

143

session, or the reverse of this situation (allow at least one recovery day between such workouts!). Two or three days are often required to complete the overcompensation process following a long run at a high-intensity level (e.g., a 50-km race). During this period, the training sessions should be at a moderate-intensity level.

If a specific TU consists of several repetitions of a specific exercise, the number of repetitions as well as the length of the rest periods must be properly regulated (see pp. 146 and 148).

Frequency of Training Sessions

The frequency of training sessions is an important factor in the recovery process that increases the performance potential. Ideally everyone should train once a day. It is better to train daily for a relatively short period at a medium-intensity level than to train once every three days three times as long and as hard. A TU of moderate to medium intensity lasting two to three times as long as a race is generally recommended for endurance-sport training. This is obviously not possible in cross-country, as the average race distance is 30 km. Naturally one should strive for long training sessions, but a distribution of several TUs of shorter duration over a week period is better than a series of TUs of overwhelming physical demand. Frequent training sessions with an excessive physical load will decrease the effectiveness of the training program. Frequent training will result in an acceleration of the recovery process and an increase in the performance potential. Beginning racers should start with a training schedule calling for four or five workouts per week. A world-class cross-country racer, on the other hand, assuming he has the necessary time, will normally train twice a day six months of the year and in the fall will sometimes train three times a day.

Cross-Country Training Methods

The previously mentioned training methods will be discussed in some detail in the next summary. The form of the physical demand and, therefore, the development of the different endurance capacities of the body can be achieved through different training methods.

Endurance Methods

These methods are characterized by a long-lasting, uninterrupted physical load. Various training methods may be instituted, depending upon the intensity desired. Also, within a single TU, the intensity may be held constant or varied. Three endurance methods are:

Continuous (constant) method: In this method the intensity level—from medium to the lower reaches of the submaximum range—is held constant throughout the workout (speed must also be held constant). This increases the general endurance capacity and is, therefore, an essential prerequisite for the development of the other endurance capabilities—but only a prerequisite. A training program limited to this method would be insufficient for the total needs of a cross-country skier—the constantly changing terrain of most courses forces the skier to change his technique, which means a change in intensity and speed. For this reason, cross-country skiing aficionados should look forward to those endurance training methods with varying tempo designed to develop special endurance capacities.

Varying method: This method consists of a regular, preplanned variance of the intensity and speed of a workout. A common example: Run one hour without interruption—ten minutes at a moderate- to medium-intensity level, then two minutes at a medium- to submaximum-intensity level. The lactic acid buildup that occurs during the two-minute intervals must then be broken down during the ten minute periods.

Fartlich: *Fart* is a Swedish word for *speed*; *fartlich* means to "play" with the tempo (and, therefore, the intensity). This differs from the Varying Method insofar as the changes in tempo are not preplanned but are rather up to the individual's mood and disposition. The changes should cover several intensity levels irregularly spaced over varying distances. Hilly terrain is ideal for the specific needs of the cross-country skier. In this method the speed should remain constant (this would be the Continuous Method on level ground) throughout the run regardless of the terrain. This constitutes a fartlich, because running on inclines demands a higher-intensity level than running on level ground at the same tempo. Running downhill is obviously easier. It is, however, more useful to vary the intensity by other means, such as striding long, flat stretches at a comfortable pace, "running" long hills, taking short, steep inclines with leaping strides, and sprinting occasional short, level stretches, and so on.

Because full utilization of all the various possibilities of endurance training results in a significant rise in the oxygen capacity, and, to a certain extent, a simultaneous increase in anaerobic capabilities and, therefore, an improvement in the special endurance capacities for skiers, this method is used universally and most frequently in cross-country training. Top racers rely almost totally on this method in the preparatory period (see page 162). Other methods, which will be described next, are useful only if this method has been practiced for some time to build a solid training base.

In these endurance methods (tempo changes included) a minimum pulse rate of 130 beats/minute (minimum effective training intensity) is maintained throughout the workout. There are other methods in which the physical load is interrupted by rest pauses.

Interval Method

The intervals (pauses) between exercises are timed so that at the end of a rest pause the pulse rate is 120 beats/minute. Naturally this allows for only partial recovery (approximately one-third of the time needed for complete recovery). Because of the body's ability to recover rapidly this is also known as the "pay period." The degree of physical demand (intensity) is designed to create the so-called oxygen-debt condition. This debt is not completely balanced by the end of the rest pause—traces of acid wastes remain in the muscles. This means that at the beginning of the next physical load the body must contend with increasing resistance caused by anaerobic (low-oxygen) conditions, forcing the body to adapt to the situation. The body basically reacts by producing enzymes designed to neutralize these acids. This process should be repeated until an advanced stage of fatigue is reached.

This method can be used for running training as well as weight training (both will be described next). In running training the individual exercises can last from fifteen seconds to two minutes (short-interval method), from two to eight minutes (middle-interval method), or from eight to fifteen minutes (long-interval method). (Pure interval training is limited solely to the short-interval method, usually at distances from 100 to 200 meters, but also to 400 meters—Freiburger Interval Training.)
meters, but also to 400 meters—Freiburger Interval Training.)

Naturally the longer the distance, the lower the intensity (short- and middle-interval training—80–90 percent; long-interval training—70 percent). The longer the distance or the higher the intensity at shorter distances, the longer the rest pause needed before the pulse rate drops back to 120 pulse beats/minute and the fewer the number of repetitions needed. As the performance potential increases, the pauses can be shortened and the number of repetitions can be increased.

During the pauses you should jog slowly. As a rule of thumb, you should jog the same distance covered by one repetition over a short distance and/or a high-intensity level.

Two short examples should serve to illustrate this method:

If a runner's best time for 400 m (level track) is 55 seconds (100 percent intensity level), he should practice at about 70–80 percent intensity (depending on conditioning, between 75 and 65 seconds) with 15–20 repetitions, and rest pauses of 1½–2 minutes. The seemingly high number of repetitions is due to the relatively low intensity level. The runner should not become fatigued until late in his workout. This type of training can also be described as an *Extensive Interval Method.* It improves the general and specific endurance capabilities of the muscles by augmenting the cardiovascular system's ability to adapt and by increasing the number of capillaries. This method can be used at an 80–90 percent intensity level (approximately 60–65 seconds per 400 m) with rest periods of 3–5 minutes to compensate for the greater oxygen-debt, with a maximum of 10 repetitions. The shorter physical demand duration is balanced by an increase in the intensity level (*Intensive Interval Method*).

This method increases the regulatory ability of the cardiovascular system and most importantly increases muscle metabolism and energy potential. For these reasons the interval methods are excellent for increasing speed and strength endurance.

In cross-country training without skis, changes in intensity level are most commonly the result of leaping-stride training or hill running (see Training Forms, pp. 154–6).This method is also used in ski training, optimally on slight inclines as opposed to level ground. If the same section of course is not used continually throughout a workout (back and forth), it is possible to institute a form of fartlick training based on the interval method. In this case, however, the intensity, distance, and length of the rest periods are hard to control.

The basic concepts of interval training are also valid in strength training with or without equipment. You should strive for the greatest possible physical demand by training under conditions more strenuous than those encountered in a race. The individual exercises (of which there are between five and ten) should be repeated either half as many times (extensive) or three-quarters as many times (intensive), depending upon personal abilities; in other words, either half as many to three-quarters as many repetitions as the maximum number of repetitions possible—as quickly as possible! After completing the desired number of repetitions for Exercise 1, there should be a pause of 30 to 45 seconds before Exercise 2 is begun, etc. After completing one full cycle of exercises, there should be a longer pause before the second cycle is begun. Depending upon the number of exercises, a workout should consist of three to five cycles *(Circuit Training)*.

A similar principle may be applied to running workouts—for example, three runs separated by short rest periods followed by a longer pause for complete recovery before the next series of three runs is begun. (This is a combination of the Interval and Repetition Methods.)

Strength endurance (of individual muscle groups) can best be improved when a portion of the workout demands full strength. To increase this maximum strength, the training must be especially "intensive," demanding relatively high exertion, long pauses, and numerous repetitions. The pauses in the Interval Method (as well as in the Repetition Method—see the next paragraph) must be basically inactive (jogging or walking), although a totally passive pause is also possible (standing, sitting, or lying). The latter is only sensible during indoor strength training because such pauses between outdoor exercises would be of little use, especially in the fall and winter when one can easily catch cold because of rapid cooling.

Repetition Method

This method differs from the Interval Method in that it requires a higher intensity level with full pauses (total recovery). The intensity level is between the top of the submaximum level and the maximum level (90–100 percent). Because of the high speeds, these repetitive runs are known as *tempo runs* (sometimes, maximum runs). This type of training creates a high physical demand on the body (primarily on the central nervous system). The body reaches an oxygen-debt state very quickly; the muscles must function under anaerobic conditons (many acidic by-products). This causes the muscles to compensate quickly for the excessive consumption of energy reserves. For this reason, this method is the most effective means of developing speed endurance. The high intensity of the training method obviously requires long rest pauses to allow the body to fully recover (the pulse rate should drop back to its rate at the start of the training session).

Tempo runs are normally from 400 meters (rarely less) to 1,000 meters. They are sometimes extended to 3,000 meters (ten minutes and longer). The number of repetitions is dependent upon the length of the individual runs: long runs may be repeated only once or sometimes not at all; short runs may be repeated up to six times. Staying within the bounds of the example given for the Interval Method, the same runner would run 400 meters in 55 to 60 seconds, jog for 10 minutes (or more), and then repeat the run five more times. Tempo runs, either on foot or with skis, should be run over level courses or, at most, over a course with flat inclines.

There are a couple of dangers related to the high physical demand of this method. It can easily prove too demanding for young skiers. For this reason, individuals sixteen years of age and under should use normal endurance training for one month before training with tempo runs, and then only cautiously (short distances at submaximum intensity!). Caution must also be practiced by adults: Frequent and intensive training without the proper general endurance training can lead to disorders in the central nervous system (at times referred to, somewhat incorrectly, as "overtraining"). If this occurs, the training load must be sharply reduced, racing and time trials must be totally stopped, and measures designed to increase the recovery processes should be instituted (massages, etc.).

Control Method

Time trials and preliminary competitions are the means by which athletes can check their level of conditioning. These are generally shorter than normal races, and the distance run must remain constant if the times are to be compared. They are run at race tempo. This method can also be used by "normal" skiers to test their form. They can, for example, run a circular course for a specific time (say, thirty minutes), counting the number of laps they complete in this time. The effects of the training program should be obvious by the increased number of laps run over the last trial. This method should not be practiced too frequently.

The full development of special cross-country endurance is best achieved through a well-balanced combination of all the methods mentioned, not by sticking to one method. The emphasis should be on endurance methods in preparation for the later training periods, which remain to be discussed.

Training Forms

Individual exercises fall under the heading of training forms. It is with the help of these exercises that the performance potential is developed. Some of these exercises may be used with all of the training methods, whereas others are suited to only one method.

These exercises may be separated into different groups on the basis of their movements in relation to race conditions. The groups—racing exercises, special exercises, and general development exercises—each is described.

Racing exercise: This exercise is intended to simulate racing conditions. Thus it must be carried out on cross-country skis utilizing all of the technique forms possible. In practice, however, these forms are quickly reduced to diagonal striding and double poling, which account for 90 percent of the exercise. The racing exercise is the most important training form for all sports, most specifically during the racing period, but also in the preparatory period. Cross-country skiing, with its seasonal and geographical dependency on snow, relies on roller skis to simulate race conditions for some training periods.

Special exercises: These include certain elements of racing movements that exercise particular muscles and muscle groups in a manner similar or identical to the demands created during racing. These exercises are designed specifically to improve the physical performance factors. They include all the running and leaping exercises used in cross-country training as well as certain strength exercises such as weight pulleys, pushups, situps, etc.

General development exercises: These include all those exercises that do not contain elements of racing movements. They are, therefore, basically exercises borrowed from other sports. The less a skier strives for high performance, the more he can rely on these exercises for physical conditioning. A ski tourer can stay fit by practicing a number of different sports that emphasize general and strength endurance (see table 00). Conversely, cross-country skiing is an excellent complement to other sports. This type of all-around sporting activity is especially useful during basic and recovery training as well as for youth-training programs. In conditioning-training programs for adults these general development exercises, specifically games and swimming, are very helpful for active recovery periods (during the transition period and during the preparatory period after a week or so of special exercises).

Cross-Country Racing and Special Exercises:	
Dry Training	Roller skis, running exercises, and gymnastics
Snow Training	Skiing

The roller ski is an ideal training apparatus—it is often the only possible means to continue training after an injury.

Dry Training

ROLLER SKIS

Despite the relatively large number of different models now available and the occasional functional differences (see Equipment, p. 23), all roller skis have one characteristic in common: roller skis (3–4 kg—6.5–9 lb.—per pair) are considerably heavier than cross-country skis. For this reason we recommend those models that roll the fastest, to ensure a rapid, easy, and "lively" movement on the roller skis. Smooth asphalt surfaces are more suitable than rough macadam; smooth surfaces are also faster and quieter, without excessive vibration. Unfortunately, the pole tips have a tendency to slip on smooth asphalt surfaces. Of course, it goes without saying that you should not train on heavily traveled streets. The street should be open, to enable the athlete to see and be seen. The roller skis should be taken off on long, steep downhills with sharp curves unless the skis are outfitted with brakes. The danger of falling, however, exists not only on downhill runs. Without sufficient practice or concentration you will find that very few roller ski models will roll in a straight line. If a ski pulls to one side or the other, you must be very adept at correcting this if you are not to

53: Roller-ski training—diagonal striding up an incline (Sigi Maier).

fall. Beginners should, therefore, start out cautiously with proper clothing (long sleeves and pant legs).

With the exception of the herringbone and skating step techniques, all other forms are possible on roller skis. The bow step is the only means of changing direction on downhills—only long, rounded curves can be navigated—although the technique is not edge to edge (see p. 115) but rather flat on the rollers.

Diagonal striding (photos 53/1 to 53/6 in this chapter) is used almost exclusively on inclines. Normal diagonal striding on level stretches, and even on flat inclines, increases the speed to such a degree that the coordination of movements becomes too difficult. Ideally, diagonal striding is used on long inclines of grades between 5 and 10 percent. However, such climbs should make up the smaller percentage of roller ski training.

The bulk of roller ski training should be taken up by double poling: no-step double poling on descents and one-step double poling on level and slightly climbing ground (photos 54/1 to 54/6). It is especially important in double poling to plant the poles properly. If the poles are planted at too sharp an angle (hand below the knee) and held behind the body for too long, the tips will probably slip out. The antislip mechanism in the roller ski ensures a steady kick under all conditions—in contrast to

54: Roller-ski training—one-step double poling (Georg Zipfel).

cross-country skis on snow. As a result, the skier must concentrate on starting his kick early to ensure that his technique at the beginning of snow training will not be sloppy. Both forms—diagonal striding and double poling—are used almost without exception for endurance training.

RUNNING EXERCISES

Running on foot was the mainstay of dry training up until around 1970. It is still important despite the introduction of roller skis. It remains the simplest, easiest, and most flexible training form for cross-country skiers.

Cross-country running: Often called "distance running," this is useful and possible almost everywhere. For the purposes of cross-country skiing, it is better to train on rolling terrain with the softest surface possible (fields or woods) than to train on narrow, flat and hard surfaces (tracks or streets, for example). Depending upon the course, the Continuous Method (more often than the Varying Method) is generally used on flat terrain, and the Fartlich Method, with all of its variations, is used on hilly terrain.

55: Leaping strides without poles (Sigi Maier).

Hill climbs: To develop the strength endurance of the leg musculature, runs on very hilly terrain (30–60 minutes) at a constant tempo are ideal. This run tends to be more of an accelerated jog than a real run, especially on steeper inclines. The skier should concentrate on kicking powerfully with his legs and emphasizing his arm movements (this motion is also known as "ski gear"). To supplement the development of the strength endurance capabilities of the arms, poles can be used. The poles should be shorter than normal for these runs as well as for leaping strides (see the next paragraph). Running at sub-maximum intensity, strong athletes can cover approximately 1,200 meters in one hour. Occasionally, these runs up and down hills at moderate to medium intensity levels (see photo 57) can last up to five or six hours and are most useful in the first stage of the preparatory period.

The preceding exercise forms are used in conjunction with Endurance Training Methods. The two following forms are used for the Interval and/or the Repetition Method.

Leaping strides: The coordination of body movements is identical to that described on page 79 for the leaping diagonal-striding method. Leaping strides may be executed with

56: Leaping strides with poles (Franz Betz).

or without poles (55/1 to 55/7 and 56/1 to 56/5), usually in a repetitive series on a (moderate) incline or in a fartlich training session. The kick should be so powerful that the kick foot leaves the ground before the lead foot makes contact with the ground (see 55/6 and 56/2). Because of the dynamic forward movement, the toes of the lead foot are pulled up and the lower leg is extended forward (see 55/3, 55/7, and 56/2, also p. 77). In executing this exercise without poles, the opposite arm (to the kick leg) is extended fully backward (55/2), whereas with poles it is only half extended (56/5). Depending upon the desired effect, a series consisting of 60–100 "leaps" (approximately 75 seconds) should be repeated eight to twelve times in Interval Training (strength endurance training) or a series of 10–40 leaps, six to eight times in Repetition Training (speed—strength). This method is very important because it is an excellent imitation of diagonal-striding movement and can be effectively continued during the winter.

Hill runs: Moderate inclines are run, using normal running form with numerous repetitions. The kick is not as powerful, the arm movement is not as pronounced, and the distance covered per stride is less than in leaping strides. For this reason, each

57: Mountain run with poles.

series can last up to three minutes in strength endurance training (Interval Method) and naturally somewhat less in speed endurance training (Repetition Training).

GYMNASTICS

Strength exercises as well as stretching and flexibility exercises are included under this heading. The following simple, effective exercises can be executed indoors or out without additional equipment. In explaining the exercise, particular attention has been paid to describing the muscle groups (arms, legs, stomach, or back) affected.

58: Arm training with weight pulleys (Hans Speicher).

Strength Exercises

The strength endurance capability of the leg, arm, and shoulder musculature should be increased through specific gymnastics exercises. In addition to these muscle groups, those used in every sport, skiing included, such as the stomach and back muscles, must be strengthened. This is best achieved through circuit training (see page 148).

Legs—Refer to diagram 13:

   (a) Practice jumps from deep-knee-bend position—a dynamic jump, bringing the arms up with the body, sinking slowly to the deep-knee-bend position.
   (b) Do one-legged deep-knee bends.
   (c) Standing on a raised step with the heels free, lift and drop heels alternately.
   (d) Standing before a stool, bench, etc., step up and down, one leg at a time.
   (e) Practice diagonal striding in place, making sure to use the arms as well.

Diag. 13. Leg exercises.

Arms—Refer to diagram 14:

(a) Pushups: normal.
(b) Pushups: with one arm in front of the other.
(c) Reverse pushups (strengthens the triceps!).

(a)   (b) l r   r l   (c)

Diag. 14. Arm exercises.

Back:

Reverse situps: Lying facedown, lift the upper body (secure feet if possible).

Stomach—Refer to diagram 15:

Situps: Lift the upper body and the legs alternately, either sideways or forward.

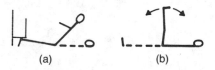

(a)   (b)

Diag. 15. Sit-ups.

To increase the difficulty of these exercises, a sack of sand may be held behind the neck and shoulders or laid over the feet.

The most effective exercises for the arms and shoulders are those using weight pulleys (58/1 to 58/4). These exercises copy the movements of double poling. If this apparatus is not available, an inner tube or a piece of elastic rope may be used by attaching one end to an immovable object and pulling against it with the arms. With this method it is possible to practice double-poling and diagonal-poling techniques.

Stretching and Flexibility Exercises (Refer to diagram 16)

(a) Extended knee bends.
(b) Leg extensions, holding the foot with the opposite hand.
(c) Lateral knee-bends.
(d) Coordinated (simultaneous) back swing of arm and leg.
(e) Alternately lifting one leg backward with the hand.

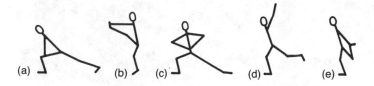

(a) (b) (c) (d) (e)

(f) Calf extenders: Lean outstretched arms onto a wall, lifting the heels alternately.
(g) Leg swings: Swing one leg at a time back and forth, while swinging the "same" hand in the opposite direction.
(h) Toe touches: With legs spread, touch opposite toes.

(f) (g) (h)

(i) Hip bends sideways.
(j) Hip circles.
(k) Arm circles forward and backward.

(i) (j) (k)

Diag. 16. Stretching and flexibility exercises.

If possible, every TU should be followed by five to ten minutes of stretching and flexibility exercises. Several training forms that are not used in endurance training must be preceded by a long active warm-up (ideally, playing games or running) and followed by a "warm-down." This is true for both dry and snow training.

Snow Training

The first few weeks of snow training should be dedicated to regaining technical skills and to generally reaccustoming oneself to skis through long outings at moderate to medium intensity levels. The various forms of conditioning for dry training are carried over into snow training. Endurance training with continuous and varying tempo, fartlich training, and interval and repetition training are all continued. Because of the decrease in friction afforded by skis and the high level of conditioning won

59: Snow training during summer in the very high elevations.

through dry training, the duration of individual TUs may be increased, initially for endurance runs and then for interval and especially tempo runs.

Tactics

A proper training program should do more than train a skier physically. A skier's performance depends not only on his physical abilities but also on his tactical-theoretical understanding of the sport (strategy). The term *tactic* is often used only in reference to individual strategies for a specific race, such as preplanned attacks and finishing kicks. This type of tactic is of little use in cross-country skiing. For example, in races with individual starts, where each competitor races against the clock, the tactic is always the same: ski as fast as possible from start to finish. Even in relay races or open races with mass starts, it would be impossible to plan on winning a race by sprinting at the finish. Of course, there are exceptions. Occasionally, it is possible for a skier who has been overtaken to "draft" the new leader until the finish, then win with a burst of speed. Whereas the original leader might not have had enough strength to hold off his pursuers, because of direct competition from his opponent, he can "overextend" himself at the end of the race to win. Drafting over a long period of time can help preserve your energy, while wearing down the lead man.

Tactic can also be understood in a broader context. It includes, for example, proper waxing. The skier who is able to combine theoretical considerations (course length, weather developments, and the like) with practical waxing experience can fully utilize his technical and physical abilities. A precautionary equipment check (is there a crack in the ski or in the plastic sole of the shoe? a tear in the pole straps? etc.) is as important as a prerace check of an unknown course (sharp turns into narrow "hidden" paths should not occur, but they do!). Even top racers who have a personal coach must be able to think for themselves. The skier's diet in general, as well as the choice of food and drink during a race, can be tactically correct or incorrect.

Best results therefore depend on the highest possible performance potential combined with the corresponding mental preparation. The athlete must have a good attitude: he must be enthusiastic about the sport. He must be disciplined, able to "exceed" himself during a race—something he can only learn in practice—even when he has little desire (for example, in the pouring rain). He must be willing to give up things for training, even when he doesn't want to. It is possible mentally to prepare an athlete with the aid of psychology (for instance, auto-suggestive training), a topic that does not, however, fit into the context of this book.

Training Periods

According to the theoretical principles of physical demand (see p. 140), we can see that performance potential increases cyclically (physical demand—fatigue—recovery—over-compensation—new demand, etc.). This wave structure of performance potential is for individual training units, as well as for increased overall performance. The breakdown and replenishing processes between two TUs, for example, or within a week (microcycle) or over a month (macrocycle), or several months (period), or a complete year, should be constantly varied by changing physical training methods.

A one-year training cycle is of particular importance. It should be designed to allow the athlete to "peak" at a specific time (for specific races). It is impossible to maintain peak form for an extended period of time. Peak form is the highest point on a long-term performance curve.

The training year is divided into three main periods:

- Preparatory period, in which form and technique are practiced.

- Competition period, in which form and technique are stabilized (races).

- Transition period, for recovery.

These periods are further divided into stages, as shown in Table 3. The dates in parentheses are those determined by the German Ski Association (DSV), and they are fine for North American skiers to follow.

TABLE 3

STAGES OF TRAINING PERIODS

Preparatory Period:

First stage	mid-May to mid-August (5/11-8/15)
Second stage	mid-August to mid-November (8/16-11/10)
Third stage	mid-November to Christmas (11/11-12/26)

Competition Period:

First stage	Christmas to mid-February (12/27-2/8)
Second stage	mid-February through March (2/9-3/31)

Transition Period:

Complete stage	April to mid-May (4/1-5/10)

Preparatory Period

First stage: In the first stage of the preparatory period the emphasis is on general endurance and strength endurance. The extent of the training should be constantly increased, with sharp differences from month to month. The intensity level should be increased more slowly, remaining in the middle range. This increases the amount of physical demand the athlete can endure as a basis for the more intensive specialized training that follows.

Second stage: The extent of training should continue to be augmented to its highest point for the year; above all, the amount of roller ski training should be greatly increased. At the same time the intensity level should be increased at a rate far greater than in the first stage. This develops general and strength endurance as well as speed endurance capacity. Approximately at the beginning of September, tempo runs should be introduced cautiously (once a week).

Third stage: For all intents and purposes, November signals the end of dry training. Only leaping strides (short series, explosive execution) and strength gymnastic training should be continued. Snow training should begin with long sessions at moderate to mid-level intensity. In November, if snow is present, more mileage is covered than during any other month!

Training sessions should remain extensive through December with an emphasis on fartlich training and tempo runs, as well as warm-up meets.

Competition Period

The design for this period depends on the specific goals set by the racer. Top skiers should peak sometime during the middle of January, stabilizing at the end of the racing season. To this end, a skier should limit himself to six to twelve races during the first stage. In the second stage the number of races should be greatly increased (approximately 15–20 races), with a corresponding decrease in the intensity of the training sessions. Because of the shorter racing season for college or weekend racers, these skiers should try to reach their peak form as quickly as possible and supplement the relatively few races available with an intensive (although not excessively so) training program, to maintain their form as long as possible. Because most of the races offered during the second stage are over longer distances, the length and/or the intensity of training sessions should not be constantly high. Long sessions, however, should occasionally be held, with a decrease in the intensity level. The total number of kilometers and hours skied (racing and training) is approximately equal to the preparatory period. A significant decrease would cause a drop in the stability of the aerobic endurance capacity.

Generally speaking, the competition period is the most important training period, although the training program must be specifically tailored to the individual skier's needs. We have a few suggestions for rounding out a racing program, consisting of one or two races per weekend with daily training during the week.

The day after the (second) race should be a "warm-down" day. The training session should not be too long and should be run at a moderate, constant speed. It is advisable to have an equally light workout before the (first) race, limited if possible to a prerace check of the course. In such workouts the skier should "insert" accelerations (lasting approximately 30 seconds) into his steady, even pace. For those skiers who race both Saturday and Sunday, one hard tempo run during the week (preferably on Wednesday) should be sufficient. If only one race is to be run per week, two tempo runs per week should be worked into the training schedule (Tuesday—Thursday or Wednesday—Friday). The tempo runs should be broken down further—for example, by dividing a longer, intense run (20 minutes) into smaller sections (3×7 minutes or $1 \times 10 + 1 \times 7 + 1 \times 3$ minutes) and then in the second run dividing the total smaller runs (10 minutes) into several short tempo runs (e.g., 5×2 minutes). The two remaining training days could be used for

TABLE 4 TRAINING YEAR—OVERVIEW*

Training Year Periods	Transition Period		Preparatory Period				
			First Stage			Second Stage	
Months	April	May	June	July	Aug.	Sept.	Oct.
Cross-country runs	30	50	45	32	45	26	28
Roller skis	15	20	25	25	20	25	25
Mountain runs		3	6	5	6	4	3
Leaping strides		10	8	7	7	7	6
Hill climbs			2	2	4	4	5
Strength exercises	5	17	14	15	18	15	13
Tempo runs						4	5
Snow training	50			14		15	15
Monthly % over the year	4	5	7	11	12	13	12

*Numbers shown represent percentages.
Note: This table refers only to training. If you wish to include racing, the monthly
Skiers who are not members of a racing team or are not living in areas receiving
snow except during the snow season. If this is the case, roller ski training should
The German National Ski Team trains, on the average, approximately 800 hours

endurance training, the first one run over a longer distance at a
relatively constant moderate intensity level, the second over a
distance approximately one-third as long, using the fartlich
training method. An increase in the amounts of fats and proteins
in the diet is recommended several days before an especially
important race. Also, a superhard (in duration and intensity)
training program should begin two or three days before the race.
These measures will result in the complete depletion of the
energy-rich carbohydrate reserves. On the last day before the
race, the training session should be light and the diet
supplemented by intensive carbohydrate consumption. This
should double the carbohydrate reserves, increasing the
performance potential for the day of the race.

Transition Period

This period could also be referred to as an "active recovery"
period. After the long preparatory and competition periods, the
body's physical and psychological powers must be allowed to
recover, without allowing the performance potential to drop too
greatly. Racing should give way to other sports as light touring,
hiking, cycling, and swimming. Light training, less frequently but
of long duration and middle intensity—not passive—is suffi-

		Competition Period			Average % of Training Form over the Year			
Third Stage		First Stage	Second Stage					
Nov.	Dec.	Jan.	Feb.	Mar.		Endurance	Methods	Dry Training
4					25			
					15			
					3			
5	7	8	5		6	Interval		
2	3				2			
7					10			
					1			
82	90	92	95	100	38			
12	7	6	6	5				

totals should be greater by about one-third.
large amounts of snow are generally unable to train on
be substituted for snow training.
per season.

cient. After four to six weeks the physical demand capacity should be increased enough to enter the new preparatory period.

Table 4 can be used as a reference chart to illustrate the amount of time you should spend on the most important training forms during the year's training. This table is based on the training schedule of the German Ski Association (DSV). The individual training forms are listed along the vertical axis and the individual months along the horizontal axis. The numbers refer to the percentage of monthly training for each form (100 percent per month).

Training Classes and Levels

The training classes and levels listed in the table on page 162 cannot be explained in detail in this book. It should be obvious training programs for children and for adults will differ and, aside from the age of the skier, the length of time one has trained is also important. A skier who has just begun to train cannot hope to start at the same level as a top racer. Whereas in many other sports such as swimming, gymnastics, and ice skating it is common for young athletes (children) to advance rapidly to top training levels, in cross-country skiing there is a much more gradual improvement in one's performance level. Generally speaking, there is a one-to-one ratio between the training classes and levels: Children = Basic Level; Youth = Intermediate Level; and Adult = Advanced/High Performance Level. Sex is relatively unimportant in determining the physical load capacity for endurance, although, recently, young girls have reached the advanced level far earlier than boys. (In 1977, two 15-year-old girls were German National Champions.) Men should plan on eight years of training to reach world-class performance levels, women about six years.

The basic characteristics of the individual training classes and levels are given in the following condensed summary.

Child (basic) training: The body's overall physical strength and motor skills should be developed; do not concentrate on the special needs of cross-country skiing.

Youth (intermediate) training: The relatively high technical performance level of the children's class should be perfected (polished form). Physical development should be continued, with an increase in training forms designed for sports, while continuing to pursue the goal of systematically increasing general physical capabilities such as endurance, strength and speed.

Adult (advanced high-performance) training: Specialized training geared to the needs of cross-country skiing, which began at the end of youth training, should be completed at this level. Conditioning, technique and tactical understanding should stabilize to allow for top performance.

This specialization process should be based on a well-planned increase of the physical demand in the intensity and extent of the training sessions as well as in the training methods and forms. It is most important that caution be exercised in increasing the intensity and that training designed to develop speed-endurance capacity (tempo runs with maximum intensity and physical load) not be introduced before the end of the youth-training level. Children up to sixteen years of age should not be subjected to heavy anaerobic demands nor to excessive strength training. The following values, based on the West German Ski Association training schedule, can be used in determining the increments in intensity and extent of training: at the end of the training level for children, 40 percent of the adult high-performance level; for youths 14 to 18 years, 50 to 70 percent; and for juniors, 18 to 20 years, approximately 80 percent.

The Thrill and Challenge of Competition

Once skiers mastered the proper techniques, they sought some means of measuring their ability against other skiers. Hence ski racing was developed. If you want to try your luck and discover how well you compare with others, try experiencing the wonderful thrill and challenge of competition.

Basically, competition in cross-country skiing takes two forms: open meets and established racing. The first is a relatively new phenomenon, whereas the second has followed a steady pattern of growth and development over the years. In this chapter, we explain the nature of both, including how you can begin competing at your own level of expertise.

Racing Associations

For years, highly organized racing under the auspices of the International Ski Federation (FIS) was a means of developing national teams, leading to ultimate competition in Olympic Games and World Championships. Every skiing nation had some organization for junior skiers that led them through beginning races to form regional teams, and finally placed them on national squads. This was how most skiers began in competition and worked their way to the big time.

In the United States, this was done under the sponsorship of the U.S. Ski Association. Junior IV racers were nine-year-old beginners, and they went on to be Junior I racers at eighteen years, then graduated into the Class A, B, or C ranks; Class A racers were selected for regional and national teams.

This system was fine while there were only a handful of dedicated cross-country skiers in the United States. As the sport grew, however, the demand for competition grew with it. In 1980, the U.S. Ski Association was split in two: one half was to be for competition only, the other for recreational skiing. All racing in the United States is now under the USSA Competition Division. The recreational ski programs are handled by the USSA Recreational Division. This separation is a complicated experiment, and it is the first time the governing body of skiing in the United States has been split, with different goals.

Pictures without words

College racers have also merged their organizations in order to provide more effective development of competition. The National Collegiate Ski Association, comprising nearly 250 college recreational ski clubs and almost that many college ski teams, merged with the Midwest Collegiate Ski Association, with 129 recreational clubs and 53 college ski teams. The new group took the name National Collegiate Ski Association, and they will continue to sponsor their own national championship. Meanwhile, larger schools belonging to the National Collegiate Athletic Association (NCAA) compete in that organization's annual national ski competition.

It's never too early to start.

Another organization, primarily devoted to teaching cross-country skiing to youngsters and to helping develop young racers, is the Bill Koch Ski League. Organized on a community and regional basis, it provides training for junior competitors under the rules of the USSA Competition Division.

Open Meets

When cross-country skiing started to become very popular in this country, some of the major insurance companies recognized the health benefits of this sport and began sponsoring amateur races. These races were open to anyone who wanted to come by and sign up. Soon other sponsors joined the bandwagon, and by the late 1970s, there were scores of open weekend races.

But the first open meets were held in Europe. Although the national ski associations were developing their organized races, there was also a demand for recreational meets. These meets began many years ago, and grew slowly in popularity until today they involve thousands of skiers.

The first open meet was the Vasaloppet, run in 1922 in remembrance of the Swedish king Gustav I Vasa. Many years passed before this type of race made its way to the Alpine lands. Then in 1965, more than one thousand contestants raced, ran, or walked from Bad Tölz toward Munich. Because of a lack of snow, the race was cut short about halfway to Munich. Until 1970, open meets were still a relatively rare phenomenon. Then this form literally exploded in all of the Alpine countries.

The number of open meets now threatens to increase indefinitely. In Bavaria alone there are more than fifty meets each season at distances of 5 to 90 km. Interested skiers can start weekend racing at the end of November and continue until the middle of March. Especially in January and February, there are at least half a dozen open meets to choose from. For those diehards who refuse to summer their skis until the very end, there is an open meet at the beginning of June on a glacier track 2,000 meters (6,500 feet) above sea level, the Glocknerlauf.

No meets go unattended. Sometimes there are only one hundred participants, sometimes ten thousand. How can this be explained? Ardent skiers could sleep in Sunday morning and still go out and ski all afternoon, closer to home, probably free from the crowds.

The main attraction appears to be the desire to perform well or, better stated, the competitive urge. Everyone can compete, whether or not he or she belongs to a club or is only a weekend athlete. It is somewhat paradoxical that the competition demanded by our society, and often avoided otherwise, is actively and voluntarily sought by these skiers. Many fall prey to the lure of inner competition or of competing against one's self, against the course, against fatigue, hunger, and thirst. It's a rare chance to push your body to its outer limits, perhaps to exceed your own abilities.

Others are drawn by the chance to compete with the pros, or perhaps with other unknowns. Others find gratification in finishing only thirty minutes behind the official winner, who is perhaps a well-known racer. No one need be ashamed of his or her technique or performance. You remain anonymous and yet at the same time are a part of the whole, caught up in the camaraderie of the race.

Some meets have an open starting time (for instance, between eight and ten o'clock), without timers, medals, or certificates of participation. But it is especially the large open meets that attract so many competitors. These meets have loudspeaker systems, starting guns, electronic timing, plaques, certificates of participation, prizes, and complete listings of the results. How many participants must fervently leaf through the lists, filled with pride at finding their "nth" placing, justifiably inspired by the truly Olympic feeling of having been there!

How Open Meets are Organized

Open meets differ somewhat depending on where they are held and who is running them. However, since the European races are the ones that have been going for the longest and involve the greatest number of skiers, let's look at how they work.

The most important cross-country open meets are shown in Table 5. Several of these meets have been combined to form special combination awards for double (or triple) winners. They are the Pustertaler Skimarathon and the Koasalauf for the Loipen trophy; the Dolomitenlauf, Marcialonga, and König Ludwig for the Alpentris; and the Finlandia Hiihto, Vasaloppet, and Alpentris for the Euroloppet. To qualify for the Euroloppet a skier must have competed in at least three of the first five races, one of which must have been in Scandinavia.

To participate in most open meets presents few if any problems. You simply arrive, compete, and leave. The larger meets, however, with their greater appeal and longer length, do require a bit of patience and understanding.

TABLE 5

MAJOR EUROPEAN CROSS-COUNTRY OPEN MEETS

Race	Country	Start–Finish	Distance (km)	First Run	Number of Participants
Pustertaler Skimarathon	Italy	Innichen–Antholzertal	60	1976	1800
Dolomitenlauf	Austria	Lienz	60	1970	2000
Marcialonga	Italy	Moena–Cavalese	70	1971	5000
Koasalauf (Kaiserlauf)	Austria	Kitzbuhel–St. Johann	42/72	1973	2500
Konig-Ludwiglauf	Germany	Ettal–Oberammergau	45/90	1968	2000
Schwarzwalder Skimarathon	Germany	Schonach–Hinterzarten	60	1974	2000
Engadin/Skimarathon	Switzerland	Maloja–Zuoz	42	1969	10,000

The first step begins with registration. Most meets have a preregistration period, ending anywhere from two months to one week before the race. However, because many of the meet organizers limit the number of entries to keep the whole affair within their control, experienced skiers preregister months in advance. The entrance fees for most meets are between five and ten U.S. dollars. For the big meets fees can be anywhere from fifteen to twenty-five dollars, and the Vasaloppet now costs forty dollars to enter. In addition, many organizers require a medical report as proof of good health.

All of the large meets are divided into racing classes. Repeat competitors must send in their time from the previous year with their registration form, so placement at the starting line can be determined. Newcomers must start at the back of the pack, unless of course they are established racers. A good time for a newcomer (or even a repeat performer) can prove valuable in determining the next year's starting position. Naturally only those competitors starting in the front line are afforded an unhindered fast race. A relatively athletic but not "qualified" skier must have great restraint (and desire) to work his way out of the pack after the start of the larger meets. Although most of

Such narrow passes are ridiculous.

A victim of the pushing and shoving? Let's hope assistance was at hand.

the rules and regulations of racing are followed in the open meets, one important rule—namely, that a skier must move aside if a faster skier wants to overtake him—is generally not observed. Occasionally a skier will step aside and allow a better skier pass, but it is much more common to see skiers push and shove their way through narrow stretches of the course. At the last Engadinerlauf, for example, more than one hundred broken skis and innumerable poles had to be replaced during the race!

On the day of the race you must rise early: Vasaloppet participants normally rise at 3 A.M. Those skiers who hope to ski with as little inconvenience as possible must take their places at the starting line as early as possible to ensure as much free room in front as possible. This means that the skier must bring extra clothing and additional waxes to the starting line, in case the conditions suddenly change. Some even bring a Thermos with a second breakfast. Naturally these things cannot be

At the finish line another mass start for the return journey

Which bag is mine? Clothing bags at the finish line.

Start of the Vasaloppet: In the back . . . .

. . . and in the first group.

carried throughout the race. Most organizers provide plastic bags, which the skiers fill, close, and somehow give to the appropriate personnel before the race. The nervous electricity filling the air before the start has led to more than one false start, unleashing an avalanche of skiers impossible to recall. The use of starting gates has proved effective in controlling the nervous and freezing skiers.

On the course, the physical strength of the contestants naturally decreases according to the distance covered and the amount of training completed. There are official food stations along the way, normally every 10 to 15 kilometers. Many participants are provided with specially prepared "secret" drink mixtures by friends and helpers. Skiers are often carried through to the finish by the enthusiastic support from the huge crowds and are often boosted by brass bands blaring in the background. Many somewhat apathetic skiers creeping along suddenly find themselves charging forward somewhat involuntarily when they hear the cheers.

Because many of the participants in the larger meets are from the ranks of the ski tourers and therefore are somewhat slow, control posts are set up around the halfway point of the course. Those who do not reach this checkpoint within a certain time limit are stopped from continuing. This is done to avoid having skiers complete the course after nightfall.

After 70 kilometers a few skiers are still fresh, the majority are tired, and a few are truly exhausted. At the end of the race even the most ambitious skiers have time to relax and enjoy the liquid and solid comforts offered (included in the entrance fee). Here, once again, confusion and excitement combine in creating a truly festive atmosphere with skiers, spectators, victory ceremonies, flag raisings, music, and general fanfare. The participant takes home the satisfying feeling of having been there, of

Personal assistance during the race.

Spectators line the course at the Engadiner Skimarathon.

A tired, but not exhausted, skier.   In cross-country jargon, he's "beat."

having tested his or her body to its limits, with the aches and pains to prove it. The starting number is a souvenir, and quite possibly there is also a certificate of participation or a medal or perhaps even a prize.

What is left for the organizers? There is little financial reward. On the contrary, because of yearly losses, the originator of this type of ski meet in the Alpine countries conducted his last open meet in Munich in 1975. Admittedly he was also forced to search continuously for snow, changing the course several times, and had to keep registration fees low as a matter of principle.

Other organizers (there are no more *private* organizers) have snow and—in the eyes of the participants—charge high entry fees. On the other hand, only half the total cost of the Koasalauf (approximately $80,000) was covered by entry fees. Other meets, such as the Engadiner, are sponsored almost totally by various interested companies, although the costs for some

Carnival time at the finish line.

services (medical and ski patrol) are borne by the organizers. Additionally, despite the long hours invested by the organizers, the total operating costs tend to be enormous. Publicity for the Engadiner meet consumed over ten tons of paper: 48,000 programs were distributed before the race (6,000 for Koasa), and a week after the race an eighty-five-page listing of all the times and places was sent to each participant—the postage alone cost some $30,000.

To enable so many skiers (at Vasaloppet, 11,000, representing eighteen countries; at Engadiner, 10,000, from twenty-six countries) to compete on one winter's day, the organizers must work throughout the year. The Marathon office in Engadin, for example, is open all but six weeks of the year, staffed by a permanent secretary; another secretary is added starting the beginning of January. This is, however, only the "tip of the iceberg." There are many voluntary functionaries active in the areas covered by the race. For the Koasa meet there are ten full-time office workers at the end of May. Starting in December, the snow on the course is prepared and maintained by Ratracs right up until race time. For the Vasaloppet, a prize committee is organized to collect prizes for the top 125 finishers at a value of $25,000. Immediately before, during, and after the race the number of workers increases drastically: 2,000 at Vasa, 600 at Koasa. To control the traffic, 200 police in helicopters, automobiles, and motorcycles are put into action (65 for Engadiner), and 30 giant transport vehicles ferry the plastic clothing bags to the finish, where some 100 workers sort them. And then the food supplies! At the "smaller" Koasalauf, where 4 radio cars constantly monitor the race, 200 workers run the 10 supply stations; 1,200 gallons of warm drink, 1,000 gallons of juice, and 2,800 bottles of beer were given out in a recent race. Food supplies included 11,000 hot dogs, 90 pounds of mustard, and 7,000 slices of bread.

Over 400 workers are needed to man the 6 control and food stations along the Vasaloppet. The food supplies available during the race (the tables alone would stretch one-third of a mile if placed end to end) included 4,000 gallons of blueberry soup, 5,000 gallons of juice, 32,000 oranges, and 22,000 sandwiches. For the meal after the race the menu included 4,500 pounds of meat and vegetables, 7,500 pounds of potatoes, and another 2,500 gallons of drinks.

There are an endless number of skiers who will stop at nothing to compete in an open meet. In one way or another, they all take it very seriously—like the seventy-year-old man from

Race organizers
served 3,750 gallons of
soup.

Garmisch who didn't start skiing until after he retired and who competed in the Vasaloppet five times before he finally covered the first 45 kilometers within the time limit and went on to finish the race, far ahead of the last skiers.

Wherever cross-country skiers gather, their conversations always lead to a round robin of frustrating, curious, strenuous, and, in the end, happy experiences. There are always skiers who after only three-year "careers" have competed in many of the most important open meets in Europe. Regardless of cost, this is their vacation—they fly to Sweden, to Finland, sometimes even to Russia to compete. Open meets have found a permanent spot in their lives.

Competition

The differences between open meets and pure racing have been gradually narrowing. This has brought about a certain flexibility within the racing sector. Many skiers, actually closer to open-meet thinking, now enter county and cup championships along with "true" racers. On the other hand, many racers, some even members of national teams, compete in most of the big open meets.

Nevertheless certain differences do remain, at the performance level as well as an official level. Every contestant in an official race must be a member of a ski club. In contrast to the mass start and except for relay races, the start is either one or at most two competitors at a time (the latter method is not used during the Olympics or world championships). The length of the course is not chosen arbitrarily but rather exactly regulated; the difficulty of the course is greater than at open meets.

Rules and Regulations

The obvious differences just noted between open meets and racing are all subject to the jurisdiction of the International Racing Rules and Regulations Committee (IWO). The course should provide a true challenge to the technical, tactical, and physical abilities of the contestants based on the standards for the specific race, without presenting excessively difficult or dangerous situations. Sharp turns, narrow passages, too many steep inclines, and dangerous conditions due to icy tracks or curves at the end of steep downhills must all be avoided, as must all interruptions of the race (crossings, etc.). The course should take full advantage of the terrain and, if possible, should run through the woods. It should combine level stretches with up- and downhill runs. If possible, these three elements should be evenly distributed throughout the course. Also if possible there should be no steep inclines at the start of the course as well as no long downhills at the finish. These rules should be most strictly followed for women's races. The course may not be repeated more than once for either world championships or the Olympics.

The course lengths prescribed for international competition, in kilometers, are shown in Table 6. There are also limitations in

TABLE 6
COURSE LENGTHS FOR INTERNATIONAL COMPETITION
(IN KILOMETERS)

	Individual Races	Relay Races
Junior girls	5	(3 or) 4 x 5
Women	5, 10	
Junior boys	15	(3 or) 4 x 10
Men	15, 30, 50	

the differences in elevation allowed: the maximum difference in elevation from the lowest to the highest point; the maximum difference in elevation from top to bottom of an uninterrupted ascent over 200 meters (that is, the highest climb); the upper and lower limits for the total course. Table 7 lists these values, as well as the color codes used to mark different courses.

TABLE 7
COURSE LIMITATIONS FOR INTERNATIONAL COMPETITION

Course	Height Difference	Highest Climb	Total Course	Color Codes Individual	Relay
5-kilometer women and junior girls	100 m	50 m	150-250 m	blue	red-blue
10-kilometer women	150 m	75 m	250-350 m	violet	
10-kilometer junior boys	150 m	75 m	250-400 m		
20-kilometer women	150 m	75 m	400-500 m		
15-kilometer junior boys	200 m	75 m	300-450 m	red	
10-kilometer men	200 m	100 m	300-450 m		green-yellow
15-kilometer men	250 m	100 m	450-600 m	red	
30-kilometer men	250 m	100 m	750-1000 m	yellow	
50-kilometer men	250 m	100 m	1000-1500 m	orange	

A daring downhill run (Georg Zipfel).   1976 Olympics: women's 5-km race.

The start and finish should be at the same elevation if possible, with a sufficiently large open area. There must be two parallel tracks for the last 200 meters going to the finish line and for double-starts at least 200 meters of parallel track at the start. Official supply stations must be set up according to the following schedule: one for a 15-kilometer race; two for a 30-kilometer race, and four for a 50-kilometer race.

There is no upper age limit for world championships. Table 8 shows the age classes for the season.

TABLE 8

AGE CLASSES FOR INTERNATIONAL COMPETITION

Competitive Category	Age Range	
	Male	Female
Schoolchildren I	7-8	
Schoolchildren II	9-10	
Schoolchildren III	11-12	
Schoolchildren IV	13-14	
Youth I	15-16	
Youth II	17-18	
Juniors	19-20	19
Seniors	21-32	20-30
Adult I	33-40	31-38
Adult II	41-50	39-46
Adult III	51-60	47-56
Adult IV	61 and over	57 and over

Note: These classes pertain for the competitive season (calendar year).

Skis are marked before the start (for championships and also for the larger open meets) to prevent skiers from illegally changing their skis during the race. During the race skiers must obey the following rules:

- Skiers must remain on the trail, passing every control station. They must cover the entire course under their own power. The whole course must be covered on skis (at least one of which must be marked). If a skier is being passed, he must move aside at the first request of the passing skiers, even if there are two parallel tracks.

- The use of pacesetters as well as other outside assistance (pushing, pulling) is not allowed, nor may anyone but the skier himself change his wax during the race. Walking on foot with skis in hand is not allowed. During the race skiers may exchange both poles but only one ski.

A skier will be disqualified if he or she:

- leaves the marked trail for a shortcut or does not pass all the control stations.

- accepts illegal assistance.

- purposefully hinders another skier or refuses to move aside when overtaken.

- covers a section of the course on foot or on two unmarked skis.

At the starting line, the skiers start individually (obligatory at world championships) or in pairs at intervals of thirty seconds. Mass starts are usually reserved for relay races (see separate additional rules for relay races, following). The feet of the skiers must be behind the starting line before the gun, the poles in front of it. Ten seconds before the start, the starter must call out, "Ready . . . 5–4–3–2–1—Go!"

The following additional rules apply to relay races:

- The starting line should be curved (covering an arc of a circle with a radius of 100 meters, the center of which should be 100 meters from the center track on the starting line). If possible, all the leadoff skiers should start next to one another, with 2 meters between them, no. 1 in the middle,

1976 Olympics: two tracks—two silver medalists (*left:* S. Bejajew, USSR; *right:* Bill Koch, USA).

no. 2 to the right, no. 3 to the left, etc. If the skiers must be started in rows, the rows should be 4 meters apart.

- The individual tracks should run 100 meters before they converge into at least three tracks. The "baton" passing zones should be well-marked rectangular areas (30 meters long and sufficiently wide). They should be in the area of the start and finish lines, on level ground. The last 500 meters of track before the passing zones and the last 200 meters before the finish line should have two lanes and be as level as possible.

- A skier can only run one leg of the relay—the starting numbers are colored (1) red, (2) green, (3) yellow, and (4) blue. The incoming skier must tag the next skier with his hand within the designated passing zones.

- A skier does not have to step aside in the last hundred meters of the race to allow another skier to pass.

International Competition

The highlights of the cross-country world are the Olympic Games (held every four years) and the Nordic Ski World Championships. The latter have been held irregularly since 1925, sometimes yearly and sometimes biyearly. Since the Second World War, the world championships have been held two years after the Olympic Games—in other words, every four years. World Championships were held in 1950—Lake Placid (USA), 1954—Falun (Sweden), 1958—Lahti (Finland), 1962—Zakopane (Poland), 1966—Oslo (Norway), 1970—Veysoke Tatry (Czechoslovakia), 1974—Falun (Sweden), and 1978—Lahti (Finland). In 1982, they will be in Oslo, Norway.

As with the World Cup of Alpine Skiing, the major international races have been combined in the past few years to form an unofficial World Cup of Cross-Country Skiing, which became official in the winter of 1977/78. It normally comprises the following twelve races in nine nations: 15-kilometer Davos (Switzerland), 15-kilometer Telemark (USA), 15-kilometer Bohinji (Yugoslavia), 30-kilometer Kastelruth (Italy), 15-kilometer Reit in Winkl (West Germany), 15-kilometer Le Brassus (Switzerland), 15-kilometer Nove Mesto (Czechoslovakia), 15- and 50-kilometer Lahti (Finland), 30-kilometer Falun (Sweden), and 15- and 50-kilometer Holmenkoll (Oslo, Norway). Each racer takes his six best races. The first twenty finishers receive points: 26 points for first place, and then 2 points less per place up to the seventh position (= 14 points) and then 1 point per position after that (twentieth place = 1 point). The World Cup Competition begins in the middle of December and ends in the middle of March. The international elite, however, continue racing into April in the numerous Scandinavian races.

As mentioned earlier in the book, the sport was dominated for decades by Norwegians, Swedes, and Finns. Then in 1954, the Soviets startled the experts by winning two races each for the men and women's events. The Soviet men didn't have another first-place finisher until 1970 (although they had become competitive with the Scandinavians), but the Soviet women have dominated the sport almost totally since 1954. (Women's events were first included in 1952.) Because of the superiority of the Scandinavians and (since 1976) the Soviet men, other Europeans and Americans found themselves out of the running. The first successes for other countries came in 1962. Since then, skiers from Italy, Poland, Switzerland, Czechoslovakia, the USA, West Germany, and, most noticeably, East Germany (two World Champions in 1974) have become competitive, although the Scandinavians and Soviets have still won more races than all the other nations combined. Table 9 (page 187) shows the record for wins by these countries.

Winning Personalities

In cross-country skiing, some racers have been able to dominate the sport for years. Here are some of the top skiers:

Thorleif Haug (Norway): This all-around athlete was almost unbeatable in his prime (six-time Holmenkoll winner since 1918). In 1924, to end his career, he won both cross-country events (50- and 18-kilometers), added a third gold medal by winning the Nordic Combination, and won a bronze in Jumping.

Veikko Hakulinen (Finland): He won three Olympic golds, three silvers, and one bronze as well as becoming World Champion three times and winning the Holmenkoll four times (1952–1960).

Sixten Jernberg (Sweden): Jernberg was the most successful skier to date, winning four gold, three silver, and two bronze medals at the Olympics and four World Championships (1956–1964).

Eero Mäntyranta (Finland): This skier won three gold, two silver, and two bronze medals, two World Championships, and the Holmenkoll three times (1960–1968).

Galina Koulacova (USSR): She was the most successful woman to date, winning four Olympic golds, one silver, and one bronze as well as five World Championships from 1968 to 1976.

Walter Demel: Demel reigned supreme for over two decades. Between 1962 and 1975 (he won his first German championship at age twenty-six) he won forty German championships. He was also one of the top international racers (third place at the 1966 World Championships for 30 kilometers; in the 1972 Olympics he was twice fifth and once seventh, just behind the winners). His colleague, Michaela Endler, won twenty-six German championships.

Despite these endurance performances (in both senses of the word), the new trend is for younger skiers to lead the sport. Previously, top international performances were given by twenty-five-year-olds and above. Now it is not uncommon to find twenty-year-olds among the top finishers. The Norwegian Ivar Formo was twenty when he won his Olympic bronze in 1972 (15 kilometers), as was the American Bill Koch in 1976, when he won the silver medal (30 kilometers). Peter Zipfel, four time

1976 Olympics: bronze medal for Arto Koivisto (Finland).

1976 Olympics: Gold medal for Nikolai Bajukov (USSR).

German champion, was also twenty in 1977, when he placed fourth in the 50-kilometer Holmenkoll race. Skiers to watch in the future include Ulrich Wehling of East Germany, the first person to win a gold medal in three consecutive Olympic Games in the same event—the Nordic Combined. Keep an eye out also for Kikoli Zimjatov of the Soviet Union, the first cross-country skier to win three gold medals at one Olympics. Juha Mieto of Finland continues to be among the world's best cross-country skiers, but he has never won a gold medal; maybe this will happen soon. The surprise team in the last Olympics, the Young East German relay team, defeated the Soviet veterans, proving that the German training system works especially well with young skiers.

This type of bunching occurs only after a mass start.
Cross-country racing in the high Alps: Geierlauf (Tyrol).

TABLE 9
DISTRIBUTION OF MEDALS IN OLYMPIC GAMES, 1924-1980*

Men's Events	18/75-km			30-km			50-km			10-km Relay			Total		
	G	S	B	G	S	B	G	S	B	G	S	B	G	S	B
Sweden	5	4	3	1	2	—	5	4	4	2	1	3	13	11	10
Norway	6	4	3	—	3	1	4	2	4	2	5	1	12	14	9
Finland	1	3	6	2	—	1	3	5	2	5	3	1	11	11	10
USSR	1	2	1	3	1	4	—	1	2	3	—	3	7	4	10
Italy	—	—	—	1	—	—	—	—	—	—	—	—	1	—	—
Switzerland	—	—	—	—	—	—	—	—	1	—	—	1	—	—	2
USA	—	—	—	—	1	—	1	—	—	—	—	—	1	1	—
East Germany	—	—	—	—	—	—	—	1	—	—	—	—	—	1	—
Bulgaria	—	—	—	—	—	1	—	—	—	—	—	—	—	—	1

Women's Events	5-km			10-km			5-km Relay†			Total		
	G	S	B	G	S	B	G	S	B	G	S	B
USSR	3	2	3	5	4	3	4	2	1	12	8	7
Finland	1	3	—	1	3	3	1	2	2	3	8	5
Sweden	1	—	—	1	—	1	1	2	1	3	2	2
Norway	—	—	—	—	1	1	2	—	1	2	1	2
Czechoslovakia	—	—	2	—	—	—	—	—	—	—	—	2
East Germany	—	—	—	1	—	—	1	—	1	2	—	1

*Not all events began in 1924. The 30-kilometer men's race was started in 1956; the men's relay began in 1936. The women's 5-kilometer was started in 1964; the women's 10-kilometer began in 1952; and the women's relay started in 1956.
†Race results for the relays include only gold medal winners for 1980 Olympic Games; this will also be reflected in the totals given.

A steep downhill run while mountaineering.

Wilderness Skiing

Although most people who are interested in cross-country skiing choose either to take up touring or racing, some brave souls consider mountaineering, or wilderness skiing. This form of cross-country skiing is the least common, and it ranges from bushwhacking through forests and over fields to mountain climbing with skis. Most cross-country skiers look upon this sport with some trepidation, and rightfully so. To climb mountains and ski Alpine slopes with normal cross-country equipment, you must be more than a cross-country skier—you must be an experienced mountain skier. But for those who are experienced mountain skiers as well as experienced cross-country skiers, the combination is actually ideal.

A quick glance at the history of skiing clearly shows that mountain skiing with cross-country equipment is not strange at all. Mountain skiers before the turn of the century (and earlier) used skis much closer in design to modern cross-country skis than modern Alpine skis (these early skis were long, with upraised tips, and, most significantly, had bindings that left the heel free). With these skis, mountaineering pioneers climbed and skied not only one mountain peak but rather whole mountain chains—for example, in 1909 Colonel Bilgeri crossed the Ötztaler and Stubaier Alps in nine days.

Because of the dominant role played by Alpine skiing in the development of skis, it is not surprising that mountain skiers began to use skis that were designed more for downhill runs than for climbing. Despite all attempts to achieve a working compromise for the problems of climbing and downhill skiing in terms of bindings and boots, the desire for ease and comfort on downhill runs tended to dominate. It is perhaps worth asking why the desire for comfort and ease in downhill skiing won out over the desire for an easier and faster means of climbing. For whatever reason no one did ask the question for quite some time.

Then, in the mid-1950s, around Innsbruck, mountain skiers (cross-country skiing was still a "Scandinavian" sport) stormed peaks and charged down slopes on normal cross-country skis. At the end of the 1960s, two Austrians on cross-country skis

At the top on cross-country skis.

raced along the high trail from Chamonix to Zermatt in two and a half days. And in the spring of 1971 two more Austrian mountain skiers crossed the Alps in forty days from Vienna to Nice (almost 1,200 miles, of which about 500 were uphill—climbing Mt. Blanc along the way), using normal cross-country equipment (light touring skis, normal cross-country bindings with an additional catch at the heel for downhill runs, and regular cross-country boots). In addition to such expeditions, mountain-climbing races, as well as races in mountainous areas, in which cross-country specialists have competed, have been common for quite some time.

In such races the skiers can climb approximately 3,000 feet in an hour—about half the time a skier using Alpine skis with the same bindings and energy would need, not to mention how long it would take to hike up a mountain. And don't think that it takes twice as long for a cross-country skier to go down the hill as it does an Alpine skier!

The reason for the better climbing ability of cross-country skis is quite simple: compact or short Alpine skis, bindings, and boots weigh approximately twenty-two pounds; cross-country equipment, about five and one-half pounds. Alpine equipment is, therefore, about four times as heavy as cross-country equipment, not to mention the comfort and flexibility of cross-country boots. The disadvantages in downhill skiing are not overwhelming. Assuming that snow conditions are not deplorable, downhill skiing with cross-country skis is manageable. If the conditions are good or ideal (a firm but giving surface, not too much powder on a hard base, and *no* ice snow [*firn*], you can traverse down the slopes leaving a track comparable to that left by Alpine skis (see also p.17). In other words, good snow conditions equalize the need for a fixed heel; the vertical mobility causes no problems, and the fear of "stepping out of the skis" while turning is minimal. And for those who look skeptically at the ankle-high Nordic boots in comparison to the calf-high Alpine boots, we ask you to think back to the Alpine boots of the early sixties or before. They provided no more support and yet Alpine skiers used them efficiently.

Of course the disadvantages should be explained. In bad snow, cross-country skiers are presented with definite problems: you can only turn with the tips; a heavy backpack becomes more than a nuisance; and your feet become wet very quickly.

On the other hand, who would want to ski when he or she knows that the snow base is jelly snow (*sulz schnee*) or a treacherous crust of frozen snow? Of course on long trips these conditions will arise—but, in spite of such conditions, the climbing advantages of weight and speed afforded by cross-country skis will more than counterbalance the disadvantages of such skis on downhill runs. Wet feet are more or less avoidable if you have good shoes, care for them properly, and wear lightweight shoe coverings and gaiters. And common sense should dictate that no one carry a heavy backpack filled with tins instead of modern lightweight foods.

In conclusion, if the snow is good and the terrain reasonable (long valleys, endless glacial runs such as in the Ötztaler), mountaineering on cross-country skis can be ideal. However, even if there are difficult downhill runs, the greater part of any trip will probably be over terrain favorable to cross-country skiing and, for this reason, the choice of equipment is not a difficult one for the experienced Nordic skier. The classic example of this is the Grosse Reibn in the Berchtesgadener, with its famous steep Loferer Seilergraben and also its 25 miles of rolling terrain, which can be covered in one day.

There are many reasons why skiers enjoy storming one or

more mountainsides in a brief time span. Most important is the ease with which you can climb on cross-country skis, not to mention the desire to ski everywhere. Mountaineering can quickly become a personal challenge. As Klaus Hoi, mountain guide and member of the two-man team that crossed the Alps, put it: "I had experienced the thrills and pleasures of Alpine skiing as a ski mountain climber. But when I discovered cross-country skiing I had the feeling that I had opened up a new door to 'Alpine bliss.' For me, cross-country skiing in Alpine terrain is a means of freeing myself from the confines of 'strict' Alpine skiing. I am able to effortlessly cover long distances and thoroughly enjoy myself on difficult downhill runs."

Need we say more? Perhaps a few words on equipment would be useful here. Naturally, for shorter excursions, superlight racing equipment would be sufficient. However, cross-country equipment specifically designed for mountaineering is available and should be used.

Skis: Use stable synthetic skis, a little wider than normal (about 55 cm) and 10 centimeters shorter (2 m for men). Several brands offer cross-country mountaineering skis with aluminum edges and greater tapering.

Boots: Cross-country boots with inner linings should be warm enough and relatively waterproof. Synthetic shoe covers and gaiters are highly recommended.

Bindings: Normal toe bindings are sufficient. A heel binding (superlight) that fits into the boot heel is available but is not a perfect solution. Many skiers design their own heel bindings. A U-shaped metal support stops the heel from sliding laterally. If the support has holes drilled in it, a strap may be run through it to help hold the boot down.

Skins: Climbing skins are generally better than wax for mountaineering. They can be looped over the front tip of the ski and strapped to the rear or looped onto the tip and temporarily glued to the sole of the ski.

References

Metric Conversion Table

Because of its European origins, cross-country skiing is primarily a metric sport. You will find skis manufactured in regular metric lengths and races given in metric distances. Here we give you a simple conversion table, in the event you are uncomfortable with these lengths. Temperatures are also noted as they relate to waxing.

TABLE 10

COMMON METRIC MEASURES FOR CROSS-COUNTRY SKIING

	Metric Measure	U.S. Customary Measure
Length	(kilometers)	(miles)
	5	3.1
	10	6.2
	15	9.3
	18	11.2
	30	18.6
	40	24.8
	50	31.0
Temperature	(celsius)	(fahrenheit)
	−30	−22
	−20	− 4
	−15	5
	−10	14
	− 5	23
	0	32
	5	41
	10	50

The Oympic Record*

The following is a breakdown by event of results in the most recent Olympic Games. Note the almost steadily decreasing times.

Men's Events

15-kilometer individual

1960	Haakon Brusveen (Norway)	51:55.0
1964	Eero Mantyranta (Finland)	50:54.1
1968	Harald Groenningen (Norway)	47:54.2

1972	Sven-Ake Lundback (Sweden)	45:28.24
1976	Nikolai Bajukov (USSR)	43:58.47
1980	Thomas Wassberg (Sweden)	41:57.63

30-kilometer individual

1960	Sixten Jernberg (Sweden)	1:51:03.9
1964	Eero Mantyranta (Finland)	1:30:50.7
1968	Franco Nones (Italy)	1:35:39.2
1972	Vyacheslav Vedenin (USSR)	1:36:31.1
1976	Sergei Savaliev (USSR)	1:30:29.38
1980	Nikolai Zimjatov (USSR)	1:27:02.80

50-kilometer individual

1960	Kalevi Hamalainen (Finland)	2:59:06.3
1964	Sixten Jernberg (Sweden)	2:43:52.6
1968	Ole Ellefsaeter (Norway)	2:28:45.8
1972	Paal Tyldum (Norway)	2:43:14.7
1976	Ivar Formo (Norway)	2:37:30.05
1980	Nikolai Zimjatov (USSR)	2:27:24.60

40-kilometer relay

1960	Finland, Norway, USSR	2:18:45.6
1964	Sweden, Finland, USSR	2:18:34.6
1968	Norway, Sweden, Finland	2:08:33.5
1972	USSR, Norway, Switzerland	2:04:47.94
1976	Finland, Norway, USSR	2:07:59.72
1980	USSR, Norway, Finland	1:57:03.46

Women's Events

5-kilometer individual

1964	Claudia Boyarskikh (USSR)	17:50.5
1968	Toini Gustafsson (Sweden)	16:45.2
1972	Galina Koulacova (USSR)	17:00.5
1976	Helena Takalo (Finland)	15:48.69
1980	Raisa Smetanina (USSR)	15:06.92

10-kilometer individual

1960	Maria Gusakova (USSR)	39:46.6
1964	Claudia Boyarskikh (USSR)	40:24.3
1968	Toini Gustafsson (Sweden)	36:46.5
1972	Galina Koulacova (USSR)	34:17.82
1976	Raisa Smetanina (USSR)	30:13.41
1980	Barbara Petzold (E. Germany)	30:31.54

15-kilometer relay

| 1960 | Sweden, USSR, Finland | 1:04:21.4 |
| 1964 | USSR, Sweden, Finland | 59:20.2 |

1968	Norway, Sweden, USSR	57:30.0
1972	USSR, Finland, Norway	48:46.1
1976	USSR, Finland, E. Germany	1:07:49.75*
1980	E. Germany, USSR, Norway	1:04:13.50

*note that the course was 20 kilometers in 1976.

---

*1980 results courtesy *Ski Racing* magazine.

Photographic Credits

Archiv Adidas: p. 19, upper left and right, lower left; p. 20, left upper and lower; p. 21, left and right. *Archiv Bergans:* p. 24, upper. *Archiv Liljedahl:* p. 22, upper right; p. 24, lower. *Archiv Sport Köpf:* p. 6, lower left; p. 58. *Archiv Swiz:* p. 45. *Archiv Trak:* p. 15; p. 18, lower; p. 19, lower right; p. 20, right. *Archiv Truma:* p. 24, lower.

Jürgen Gorter, Munich: p. ii. *Sidonium Holm,* Munich: p. 173, middle and lower; p. 177. *Toni Landenhammer,* Reit im Winkl: p. x; p. 16; p. 17, upper and lower; p. 18, upper left and right; p. 22, upper left and lower; p. 63; pp. 156–57, lower. *Gustav Maier,* Munich: p. 23; pp. 112–13; pp. 116–17; pp. 122–23; pp. 124–25; pp. 126–27; p. 151. *Rolf Arne Odiin,* Norway: p. 7, lower left; p. 27, lower left; p. 179, left and right; p. 181; p. 184; p. 185. *Georg Sutter,* Nesselwang: pp. 154–55.

Photographs by the authors: *Sigi Maier:* p. 7, lower right; p. 10; p. 12, lower right; p. 27, lower right; p. 34; p. 45, lower; p. 51, left and right; p. 54; p. 55, left and right; p. 57; pp. 60–62; p. 67; pp. 70–109; p. 110 and 111 (upper); p. 119; p. 120; pp. 129–33; p. 168, upper and lower; p. 172, upper and lower; p. 173, upper; p. 174–75; p. 186, upper. *Toni Reiter:* p. ii; p. 5; p. 6, upper and lower right; p. 7 upper; pp. 8–9; p. 11; p. 12, left; p. 13; pp. 29–30; p. 50; p. 53; p. 55, middle; pp. 64–65; p. 111, lower; pp. 152–53; pp. 154–55, upper; p. 156, upper; p. 160; p. 186, lower left and right; p. 188; p. 190

The diagrams were designed by Sigi Maier.

Bibliography

Astrand, P.O. and K. Rodahl. *Textbook of Work Physiology.* New York: McGraw-Hill, 1977.

Brady, Michael M. and L.O. Skjemstad. *Ski Cross Country.* New York: Dial Press, 1974.

Brower, David, ed. *The Sierra Club Manual of Ski Mountaineering.* New York: Ballantine Books, 1969.

Caldwell, John. *The New Cross-Country Ski Book.* Brattleboro, Vt.: Stephen Greene Press, 1971.

FIS. *The International Ski Competition Rules, Book II, Cross-Country and Nordic Combined Events.* Bern: FIS, 1971.

Lederer, William J. and Joe Pete Wilson. *Complete Cross-Country Skiing and Ski Touring.* Second Edition. New York: Norton, 1975.

Novosad, J. and J. Waser. Skisport. Moscow, 1975.

Ski Touring Council, Inc. *Ski Touring Guide.* New York: Ski Touring Council.

Tejada-Flores, Lito, and Allen Steck. *Wilderness Skiing.* San Francisco: Sierra Club Totebook, 1972.

INDEX

absolute strength, 137–38
adhesive waxes, 41
adult training and competition,
  166, 180
aerobic endurance, 138, 143
aggression, 30
agility, 140
Alpentris competition, 170
Alpine skiing, 4, 8–11, 17, 44,
  71, 119, 121, 169,
  189–92
amorphous snow, 39–40, 42
anaerobic endurance,
  138–39, 143
arm/pole action, 62, 66–68,
  79–80, 87–88
Australia, 11
Austria, 8, 170–71, 189–91

Bad Tölz-Munich race (1965),
  169
Bajukov, Nikolai, 194
balance, 140
base form, 59, 61
base wax, 44
basic endurance, 138
baskets, 20
Beraur, Hans, 7
Bilgeri, Colonel, 189
Bill Koch Ski League, 169
binder wax, 44, 54–55
bindings, 3, 14, 16–18, 192
Birkebeiner race, 2
blood pressure, 26–27, 139
bogenlaufen, 93, 118
bogentreten, 115
Bohinji race, 182
boots, 14, 18–19, 192
bow running, 118–19
bow steps, 93, 115–18
Boyarskikh, Claudia, 194

Bra, Oddvar, 130
Brusveen, Haako, 193
Bulgaria, 187

California, 4, 8
calorie requirements, 28, 32
camber (tension) 15–16
can waxes, 46
carbohydrate requirements,
  28, 32, 164
child training and competition,
  166, 180
Christiania (Oslo) race (1868),
  3
circuit training, 148
classes, training, 165–66
cleaning and preparation of
  skis, 49–51
climbing zones, 16
clothing, 21–22, 31
coarse-grained snow, 37–38
Colorado, 5
competition, 167–87
competition periods, 163–64
conditioning, 134–40
constant method, 145
continuous method, 145
control training method, 149
Cortina d'Ampezzo, Olympics
  at, 8
courses, racing, 12, 48,
  178–82
cross-country running, 153
"cross-country thumbs," 30
crystalline snow, 39–40, 42
Czechoslovakia, 7, 182–83,
  187

damp snow, 38
Dartmouth Outing Club, 4,
  11–12

Davos race, 182
"dead" skis, 41
demands, of training, 140–44
Demel, Walter, 184
diagonal striding, 60–68,
    81–88, 90–91, 106–10,
    128
Dolomitenlauf race, 170–71
double pendulum steps, 92
double poling, 93–106, 128
downhill forms, 59, 119–21,
    191
downhill running, 119–21
dry snow, 38
dry training, 150–59
dry waxes, 41–42, 46–47,
    53–55
Durango, Col., 11
duration, 143

"easy chair" position, 121
elevation changes, 48
Ellefsaeter, Ole, 194
end form, 59, 62
Endler, Michaela, 184
endurance, 138–39, 143
endurance training methods,
    144–46
energy sources, 28, 139
Engadin Skimarathon race,
    171–72, 175–76
Euroloppet race, 170
evaporation (sublimation), 37
exercises, 149–60
extensive interval training, 147
extent of demand, 143

fall line, 119–20
Falun race, 182
Falun World Championships
    (1954, 1974), 182
fartlich, 145–46, 164
fatigue, 138–39
fats and fatty acids, 28, 32,
    164

fine-grained snow, 37–38
Finland, 3–4, 7–8, 170, 177,
    182–83, 185, 187,
    193–94
Finlandia Hiihto race, 170
firn, 191
flexibility, 139
Formo, Ivar, 184, 194
forms, training, 149–60
four-beat steps, 91–92
France, 190
Freiburger interval training,
    146
frostbite, 31
frozen snow, 10–11, 37–38,
    191

gaiters, 22
general endurance, 138–39
Germany (East and West), 4,
    8, 25, 129, 162, 165–66,
    169–71, 182–85, 187,
    194–95
glide phase, 35, 41–43, 62,
    66, 76–78, 86
glide zones, 16, 40
Glocknerlauf race (1976), 68,
    169
gloves, 21–22
glucose requirements, 28
glycogen reserves, 28, 139
granular snow, 10, 12, 37–38
gravity-shift point, 63, 69
Greenland, 4
Grenoble, Olympics at,
    193–95
grips, 20
Groenningen, Harald, 193
Gusakova, Maria, 194
Gustafsson, Toini, 194
Gustav I. Vasa, 2, 169
gymnastics, 156–59

Haakon IV, 2

Hakulinen, Veikko, 183
half-herringbone technique, 112
half-skating step, 115
Hamalainen, Kalevi, 194
handgrips, 20
Harald I, 2
hard waxes, 41–42
Haug, Thorleif, 183
health factors, 25–34, 135–37, 139, 164
heartbeat and heart volume, 26–27, 33, 139
herringbone technique, 110–12
Heynen, H.P., 25
hill climbs, 154
hill runs, 155–56
Holmenkoll race, 3, 182–83, 185

impregnating wax, 44
injuries, 30–32, 34
Innsbruck, Olympics at, 8, 14, 129, 193–95
intensity of demand, 141–42
intensive interval training, 147
International Racing Rules and Regulations Committee, 178
International Ski Federation, 167
intervals, 146
interval training method, 146–48
Italy, 5, 8, 170–71, 182–83, 187, 194
Iverslokken race, 3

jelly snow, 69, 191
Jernberg, Sixten, 183, 194
jumpsuits, 21

Kaiserlauf (Koasalauf) race, 170–71, 175–76

Kastelruth race, 182
kick phase, 35, 40–42, 62–64, 72–75, 83
Klause, G., 129
klister, 40–42, 47–48, 53–56
Koasalauf (Kaiserlauf) race, 170–71, 175–76
Koch, Bill, 14, 169, 184
Koivisto, Arto, 68
Kolchin, Pavel, 7
König-Ludwiglauf race, 170–71
Koulakova, Galina, 8, 184, 194

Lahti race, 182
Lahti World Championships (1958, 1978), 182
Lake Placid, N.Y., Olympics at, 4–5, 14, 194–95
leaping strides, 154–55
Le Brassus race, 182
levels, of training and competition, 165–66, 180
Loipen competition, 170
Loppet League, 2
Lundbäck, Sven-Ake, 130, 194
lung capacity, 27–28, 139

Madison Square Garden, N.Y., 4
Magnus, Olaus, 2–3
Magnusson, Thomas, 88
Mäntyranta, Eero, 183, 193–94
Marcialonga race, 170–71
maximum strength, 137–38
melting, 37–38
metabolism, 27–28, 33, 139
methods, training, 144–49
metric system conversions, 193
mid-lived endurance, 138–39

Midwest Collegiate Ski
    Association, 168
Mieto, Juha, 185
mineral requirements, 32
mittens, 21
mobility, 139–40
motor skills, 139–40
"mousetrap" bindings, 3, 16
movement, fundamentals of,
    68–81
Munich International Ski Meet
    (1965), 8
muscle development, 26–28,
    31–32, 138–39, 146

Nansen, Fridtjof, 4
National Collegiate Athletic
    Association, 168
National Collegiate Ski
    Association, 168
New Hampshire, 4, 11–12
Nones, Franco, 194
Nordic Ski World
    Championships, 182–83,
    185
Norway, 1–4, 7–8, 130, 170,
    182–84, 187, 193–95
Nove Mesto race, 182
Novosad, J., 68–69, 75

Oberholzer, 133
Olympic Games, 167, 170,
    177–78, 182–85, 187,
    193–95
  1932 at Lake Placid, 4–5
  1956 at Cortina d'Ampezzo,
    8
  1960 at Squaw Valley, 8,
    193–94
  1964 at Innsbruck, 8,
    193–94
  1968 at Grenoble, 193–95
  1972 at Sapporo, 194–95
  1976 at Innsbruck, 14, 129,
    194–95

  1980 at Lake Placid, 14,
    194–95
one-step double poling,
    99–106
open meets, 169–77
"open" racers, 69
Oslo (Christiania) race (1868),
    3
Oslo World Championships
    (1966), 182
overall speed in movement,
    138
oxygen consumption, 27–28,
    33, 138–39, 146

paraffin wax, 44
pauses, 146
pendelgang, 91
pendelschritte, 89
pendulum gait, 91
pendulum steps, 89–93, 106
performance factors, 137–40
periods, training, 161–65
Petzold, Barbara, 194
Poland, 182–83
poles and poling, 13–14,
    19–20, 23, 80, 93–96
powder snow, 10–12, 37–38,
    191
pre-kick phase, 62–63,
    69–72, 83
preparation and cleaning of
    skis, 49–51
preparatory periods, 162
protein requirements, 28–29,
    32, 164
psychological aspects, 29–30,
    32
pulse rate, 26–27, 139
purchase, 40–41
purchase wax, 44, 46
push with the arms, 62, 66–67
Pustertaler Skimarathon race,
    170–71

racing
  associations, 167-69
  exercises, 150
  techniques, 59
  waxing for, 56-58
racing skis, 15
recovery periods, 143-44,
  146
reflex speed, 138
Reit im Winkl race, 182
repetition training method,
  148-49
Repo, Juhani, 92
Riva Ridge, Col., 5
roller skis, 11, 23, 151-53
Rue, Jon Thoresen, 4
rules and regulations, 178-82
running exercises, 153-56
running forms, 59, 119-21

Sapporo, Olympics at,
  194-95
Savaliev, Sergei, 88, 194
Schwarzwalder Skimarathon
  race, 171
seasonal changes, 48
Seefeld, Olympic competition
  at, 14
short-lived endurance,
  138-39
Siebert, Pete, 5
skating steps, 112-15
Ski Association (U.S.), 167,
  169
Ski Association (West
  German), 162, 165-66
skins, 192
skis, 1-3, 9, 12-16, 180
  cleaning and preparation of,
    49-51
  roller, 11, 23, 151-53
  waxing of, 51-56
  for wilderness skiing, 192
Skisport, 68

Smetanina, Raisa, 194
snow, 9-12, 36-40, 42, 191
snowshoes, 1-2
snow training, 150, 159-60
socks, 21
soft waxes, 41-42
Soviet Union, 7-8, 68, 177,
  183-85, 187, 194-95
"special" (or "special
  competition") endurance,
  139
speed, 138
speed endurance, 139
speed strength, 138
Sport Federation (West
  German), 25
Squaw Valley, Calif., Olympics
  at, 8, 193-94
stay power, 139
stopping, 121
strength, 137-38
strength endurance, 139
stride type, 59
striding. See diagonal striding
style, 128-29
sublimation (evaporation), 37
sulzschnee, 69
Sverr, 2
Sweden, 2, 4, 7-8, 129-30,
  169-70, 177, 182-83,
  187, 194-95
swing of the arms, 62, 67-68
swing phase, 62, 64-66, 76,
  83, 86
Switzerland, 171, 182-83,
  187, 190, 194

tactics, training, 160-61
techniques, 59-133
Telemark race (Norway), 3-4,
  11
Telemark race (U.S.), 182
tension (camber), 15-16
terrain, 9-12, 59, 106

Thoma, Georg, 8
Thomson, John A., 4
three-beat steps, 90–92
tips, 20, 23
Todtnau ski club, 4
touring, ski, 8–9, 59
touring skis, 15
tracks, 10, 12–13, 41, 48, 59, 106
training, 23, 31–33, 134–66
  classes and levels, 165–66
  demands, 140–44
  forms, 149–60
  methods, 144–49
  performance factors, 137–40
  periods, 161–65
  tactics, 160–61
training units (TUs), 143–44, 159, 161
transition periods, 164–65
transitions, 106–10
turning, 121
TUs. See training units
Tweedy, Penny, 5
two-beat steps, 90–91
two-step double poling, 106
Tyldum, Paal, 194

underwear, 21
United States Ski Association, 167, 169
uphill forms, 81–88, 110–12

Vail, Col., 5
varying method, 145

Vasaloppet race, 2, 169–72, 176–77
Vedenin, Vyacheslav, 7, 194
Veysoke Tatry World Championships (1970), 182

warm-ups and warm-downs, 159, 162–64
Waser, J., 68
Wassberg, Thomas, 129, 194
wax skis, 15, 35
waxes and waxing, 3, 9–10, 14–16, 35–58
waxing accessories, 49
waxless skis, 15, 35
Wehling, Ulrich, 185
wet snow, 38
Widia tips, 23
wilderness skiing, 189–92
Wisconsin, 2
World Cup and World Championships, 8, 129, 167, 182–84
World War II, 5

youth training and competition, 166, 180
Yugoslavia, 182

Zakopane World Championships (1962), 182
Zimjatov, Nikolai, 185, 194
Zipfel, Georg, 83, 88, 133
Zipfel, Peter, 83, 88, 184–85
zones of a ski, 16, 40

Olympic Gold Medalist Jean-Claude Killy and French ski coach Honoré Bonnet cover everything from beginning instruction to après-ski camaraderie. Sequence photos show how to do the snow plow, christies, turns, sidesliding, wedelns, avalement, and more. **$12.95** hardcover

Style is the subject of this book. It begins where most ski books leave off — with parallel skiing — and teaches the techniques that make a competent skier into a very good skier. **$6.95** paper

Chester Barnes' object in writing this book was to describe methods of play as he has come to understand them as a champion, and to encourage newcomers to try their hand at this exhilarating game. **$1.95** hardcover

Expert Celia Brackenridge shares her knowledge and skills in this fast-paced game. Intended to teach an effective way of playing lacrosse, this book looks at all aspects of the sport in relation to the game and game situations, rather than isolation. **$4.95** hardcover

An international team of 12 boating authorities wrote this book that takes in all aspects of sail and power boating including history, theory, navigation, safety, construction, and more. **$14.95** cloth

A champion and an experienced coach with knowledge of all aspects of field hockey, Rachael Heyhoe Flint gives sound advice on the techniques and method of play, which is enhanced by excellent action photos. **$4.95** hardcover

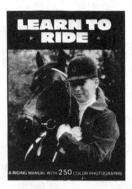

Now anyone can predict the weather...

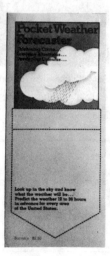

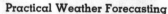

Practical Weather Forecasting
by Frank Mitchell-Christie; $9.95 hardbound
This comprehensive weather guide explains all about the various factors that cause different types of weather. It includes such unique features as Weather at Sea, which discusses wave patterns and heights, and Making Your Own Weather Charts.

Pocket Weather Forecaster $2.50
Simply by matching wind and cloud conditions you can forecast the weather up to 36 hours in advance, anywhere in the United States.

At your local bookseller or order direct adding 10% postage plus applicable sales tax.
BARRON'S
Woodbury, New York 11797

Prices subject to change without notice.

THE BIG BOOK OF
MOUNTAINEERING

T o the ancients. the mountains were the abode of the gods: today. in less reverent times. they stand as the ultimate challenge to the human will.

This is a book about the mountains. and about the special breed of men and women who live with a magnificent obsession: to climb, to struggle. to **prevail** over the loftiest and most defiant peaks. knowing all the while that they might never return. It is a book of surpassing beauty — substantial in size. luxurious to the touch. filled with stunning color photographs of the mountaineer's aerial realm. including a number of spectacular double-page spreads.

The Big Book of Mountaineering is more than a superb coffee-table showpiece. Its pages are distinguished by engaging and intelligent articles on the mountains and the people who climb them. Written by an international team of experts headed by journalist-mountaineer Bruno Moravetz. **The Big Book of Mountaineering** covers a diverse range of intriguing subjects. from mountain geology. flora. and fauna to the significance of mountains in religion. art. and literature. But the heart of the book is devoted to adventure — thrilling accounts of historic climbs in the great mountain ranges of the world. From the Alps. the Himalayas. the Andes. and the Sierras come stories of incredible perseverance in the face of death. stories of triumph and disaster that make unforgettable reading. And these stories are all the more compelling because the writers have actually been there.

10-7/8″ x 13-15/16″
288 pages
112 pages of
full-color illustrations
$49.95 cloth

9649

796.93 Maier, Sigi
MAIER
           Cross-country
                  skiing

$4.95 paper

	DATE		
Joseph			
DEC 1 1983			
OCT 31 1985			
Fortin			
JAN 1 5 1987			
MAR 5 1992			